Take My Hand

Take My Hand

A Theological Memoir

ANDREW TAYLOR-TROUTMAN

RESOURCE *Publications* · Eugene, Oregon

TAKE MY HAND
A Theological Memoir

Resource Publications
An Imprint of Wipf and Stock Publishers
199 W. 8th Ave., Suite 3
Eugene, OR 97401
www.wipfandstock.com

ISBN 13: 978-1-61097-684-8
Manufactured in the U.S.A.

Dedicated to Ginny, Matthew 6:21
In memory of Granddad, Romans 1:16

Contents

Foreword

WHEN I WAS A young boy, I would often follow my father to his workshop after dinner. Out in his old, wooden shed, I would watch him tirelessly take things apart and slowly put them back together. Along the way, he would offer comments and reflections on why it is important to care for and repair what you have. In spite of his tutelage, I did not really learn how to repair lamps, build a bookcase, or work on a car. What I did learn by spending time with him in his workshop was about the way he viewed life and how he viewed these tasks in relationship to his life. In many ways, these are far more important lessons than how to replace a socket in a broken lamp or change the sparkplugs in a car. What this time with my father gave me was a clearer sense of my father's identity and his own understanding of vocation.

When I read through the pages of Andrew Taylor-Troutman's memories of his first year as a pastor, I have a similar feeling of insight and discovery. This is the story of a growing sense of belonging between a pastor and a congregation and a deepening satisfaction with the daily tasks, challenges, and opportunities of a pastor in the context of a particular community. This is precisely why I think that this is a wonderful book not only for new pastors, but especially for members of congregations. Each chapter presents a sermon as a series of ongoing conversations: between a preacher and a text; between a preacher and a congregation (and broader community); and between a text and an ever-changing context. This lively conversation locates the weekly task of preaching within the daily events of life. Here, the pulpiteer is forced to come down from his/her high and lofty location and struggle with texts in light of the dynamics of congregational life. And what Andrew so carefully shows are the ways that these conversations also include the ghosts of the past that so often hover over this process in our churches.

Here, in a small, rural, historic church in western Virginia, the art of preaching as dialogue comes to life. As one who teaches preaching, I am delighted to have this real-life memoir of a recent student of mine. No matter how hard I try, I cannot possibly construct the richness, diversity, and complexity of congregational life that provides the context in which each week ministers rise up from the middle of congregations in order to speak of the possibility of encountering God in these odd stories which we call Holy Scripture and in the midst of our busy and messy lives. Even more important, in my estimation, is the ability of the minister to consistently model whether or not there is any truth in or connection to the claims that the gospel makes on our lives. On all of these accounts, this memoir succeeds in the art of practicing what it preaches.

Preaching as an ongoing dialogue and a relationship with a particular congregation are at the heart of what parish ministry is all about. The conversations that begin in our living rooms and over our dining tables shape how we hear and respond to Scripture and the ways that we live out this gospel in our community. These dialogues accompany us to our hospital rooms and support us in times of crisis. Here, Andrew points us to ways that all of us struggle to make sense of texts and contexts and how we can live them out together in a community of faith. At the same time, Andrew models for us how, in the midst of these conversations and challenges, we can grow into faith practices that sustain us and give us a deeper sense of awareness of our own identity and vocation.

Andrew shows how the simple, yet profound act of framing pastoral conversations as questions opens the door to discovery: What have you been praying about lately? Similarly, the art of preaching centers around a question: Where can we experience God in this text? Such an approach invites us all into the lifelong process of looking for and discovering God's presence in our lives.

Several years ago when I was preaching each week in the congregation where I served as pastor, my spiritual advisor likened the work of writing sermons to the work in the shop that my father loved to do. Whether it was repairing a broken lamp so that light would once again shine, hammering together wood to support our family's vast library, or slowly and lovingly restoring his old Model A Ford, these were the tasks that my father worked on while I listened to him reflect on life. I learned to think of my own sermons in similar ways: as the careful work of one who listens to texts, to the voices in the congregation and community, and to the ghosts of the past that haunt every church I know. In the end, this work is primarily a work of love: to care for these people in this particular place and time as one reflects out loud on the possibility that this text will help us see our lives together in a new way.

So I happily commend this book to you as one that will bring you insights into the difficult and demanding work of preaching. Even more importantly, though, I recommend this book as one that shows us ways to live out our calling as disciples of Jesus Christ in our own particular communities of faith.

Paul Galbreath
Professor of Worship and Preaching
Union Presbyterian Seminary
Richmond, Virginia

Acknowledgments

Philippians 1:3

I WOULD LIKE TO thank my parents, Craig and Anna, and my parents-in-law, Chuck and Marilyn, for their support and encouragement throughout this process. They all graciously read early drafts and *Take My Hand* is better because of their guidance. I am also grateful for the interest shown by my brother, John, my sister-in-law Kelly, and my brother-in-law, Drew. Thanks to Paul Galbreath, not only for writing this foreword, but for reading a rough draft and offering helpful advice. Also Carson Brisson, Beverly Zink-Sawyer, and Frances Taylor Gench are all former seminary professors who have continued to be encouraging of my ministry. I hope that Carson reads the multiple allusions to his work as emblematic of my respect for him. I wish to thank all of the participants at the 2011 *Believing in Writing* workshop, including the staff at the Collegeville Institute, and especially Michael Dennis Browne for his attentive reading of chapters four and seven. Valerie Cooper pulled me through the program at UVA, and she inspired me to write as both a pastor and an academic. Finally, so many people have been supportive at New Dublin! As I say every Sunday, I am blessed to be here. This book is an extended "thank you" to each one of you. But I'd like to thank Richard and Frances by name for saying, "We want you and Ginny here."

And speaking of Ginny, I am forever grateful.

Introduction

It Seems to Me

THE PURPOSE AND FORMAT OF THIS BOOK

NEW DUBLIN, VIRGINIA WAS founded by settlers from the "old" Dublin across the pond in Ireland. It is said that our founders gazed upon the New River valley and felt that God had called them to settle *here*. In 1769, they built a little church on a hill. Presumably God had something to do with that as well, though in the local lore, New Dublin Presbyterian Church was actually the request of the fiancée of a local landowner. She refused to travel to the "back country" unless she could attend a Presbyterian church!

While the town of New Dublin was eventually shortened to just Dublin, life has remained remarkably consistent from those first congregants to the people that I would serve, despite a vastly different world around them. As evidence of this consistency, one church leader has been a member of four different presbyteries over the course of his lifetime, yet he has lived in the *same house* for eighty years. Farming has remained a way of making a living and, just as importantly, a way of life. This is a place and a people with deep roots.

While I have a strong connection to my heritage as well, I have moved quite often over the course of my young life. In fact, my first visit to Dublin took place less than four months after my most recent move to Charlottesville, Virginia. In August of 2009, my wife and I bought our first house and made plans to settle down. I was a student at the University of Virginia, and she served as a chaplain in the same university's hospital system. It was a natural progression for a young married couple both recently graduated from Union Presbyterian Seminary in Richmond. As we moved just seventy miles down the interstate, we expected to continue our careers in the academy and the hospital. Charlottesville was the place where we pictured growing our family.

That *was* our plan.

On January 17, 2010, I accepted the call with Ginny's blessing to live and work at New Dublin Presbyterian Church.

So, what in the world happened? Why did this call to ministry happen? In fourteen chapters of reflections and sermons, this book reflects my exploration of these questions. *Take My Hand* is an invitation to see New Dublin Presbyterian Church from my eyes and, as a consequence, understand something about how I view my calling. I am grateful to explore my first year as a pastor with you. But before I lead you along this journey, let me share a little more about myself and this book. I want you to trust your guide.

I am the eldest son of a pastor. I spent most of my childhood and my entire adolescence in the same church. At my dad's church, Raleigh Moravian, there were plenty of people who felt that the apple didn't fall too far from the tree. One evening at youth group, when I was being obnoxious in ways seemingly endemic to preacher's kids, one of the leaders pulled me aside. He told me that I had better behave because I would be leading my own youth group one day. I laughed and ran away—no way was I going to be a pastor!

As I grew up, however, I gradually took steps into the ministry. I was active in my high school youth group; I became a volunteer leader of youth group in college; I was employed as a full-time youth director after college. I attended Union Presbyterian Seminary, where I learned that the famous King James translation of Psalm 23 about the "goodness and mercy" that "shall *follow* me all of the days of my life" is actually describing a God who actively and intensely *pursues* humankind. This God does not walk behind us in a leisurely stroll; the Hebrew verb for "follow" describes the force of a bird of prey, swooping down from above (Lam 4:19). Each of my steps into ministry may seem tame, but I believe my life is evidence of the *hot* pursuit of God. I have never heard a voice from heaven nor seen a light from above nor even dreamed of a commissioning vision. But despite a lack of supernatural phenomena, I do believe my calling to the parish was by divine guidance. More and more with each passing experience in ministry, it seems that a pastor is a vital part of who I am.

At New Dublin Presbyterian Church, there is a sign that points to our church. Underneath the name of the church hangs another sign that identifies me as a "pastor." The pastor used to be known as the "parson," which is actually derived from the Old English word for *person*. I find this etymology significant because I feel that my vocation is truly a part of me. I am a person who is called to this position at this point in my life. Though I've run away from such a calling before, God has not given up pursuit. I consider it a great honor that my name is on that church sign today.

The following pages represent what I've learned as I continue to grow into my profession and my vocation. As I invite you to take my hand, I have structured this book in the manner of my experience. I begin each chapter with a reflection on a particular aspect of parish life. These insights introduce themes I will explore at the end of each chapter in a sermon. While I have made some changes for general use, I preached a version of each sermon at New Dublin. Therefore the format of this book reflects, not only my thoughts about ministry, but demonstrates an evolving understanding, roughly month-by-month, through the first year of being a pastor. For this reason, I have subtitled my work as a *theological* memoir. *Take My Hand* is a look back at a specific time in my life explicitly through the lens of my graduate education and my own faith. In its own small way, I hope this book is able to convey something of the mysterious process of writing a sermon by demonstrating how the preacher's work on Sunday morning grew out of his or her experience the previous weeks, months, and years.

While some material is explicitly theological, I want to be clear that this book is a *memoir*. It is about real-life relationships. As such, the following pages include moments that are deeply personal. Some passages may even raise an eyebrow! In brief, I must say that I have received permission from every person either directly named or alluded to in this project. I am grateful beyond words to each individual whose permission enabled me to tell a specific part of the story that we are all writing together. Believe me, the last thing I want to do is compromise the bonds of trust that were formed during my first year of ministry. Furthermore, the people of New Dublin have taught me a great deal, but I do not wish to suggest that I view these relationships as mere object lessons. I want my reader to come away from the book with the clear understanding that I have respect for these parishioners as friends and fellow disciples. As you walk with me, I hope that you, too, will come to appreciate them. Despite the risks of disclosure, this book must be personal because I preach to people I personally know. As the eternal Word became flesh in Jesus Christ, so our faith as his disciples is embodied in our community.

Before we embark on our journey, I want my readers to know that New Dublin is good listening congregation. After I preached for a few weeks, many noticed that a particular phrase often crops up in my sermons: *it seems to me*. Initially I employed this phrase as an introductory formula, as a way to emphasize the claim that follows. While the phrase began as a mere stylistic flourish, I realized the importance of these words after a few months of preaching. "It seems to me" is like a disclaimer that whatever follows is my opinion. I think such humility is necessary when one deals with the proclamation of ancient texts to a modern audience. I am theologically trained, but that does not mean that I am the judge who renders the final verdict in all matters of interpretation. I like the way Martin Buber put it: "I am no philosopher, prophet, or theologian, but a man who has seen something and who goes to a window and points to what he has seen." Let me be clear that the opinions expressed throughout this book are my own. As I've already warned you about deeply personal material, I also want to state that some of my conclusions are controversial. You are invited to take my hand; you are not asked to like every place I take you or agree with everything I say!

In the Reformed tradition, God's word is communicated by an act of the Holy Spirit working through the preacher. Like treasures contained in clay jars, God uses the very mortal words of pastors to convey the eternal Word to other humans, "so that it may be made clear that this extraordinary power belongs to God" (2 Cor 4:7). Tom Long notes, "Christ is not present because we preach; we preach because Christ is present."[1] It follows, then, that Christ is present with all of us on Sunday morning, not just the preacher. I hope that "it seems to me" invites listeners and readers to engage in their own process of interpretation. On Sunday morning, I want people to listen deeply to my words for assurance and for challenge. As I wrestle with Scripture, theology, and ethics, I invite you to find meaning for your life and draw your own conclusions.

---

1. Long, *Witness of Preaching*, 16.

Karl Barth once said that every person comes to church on Sunday morning with one question in mind: is it true? "Truth" in this sense is deeper than any personal opinion because this "it" is bigger than any one person. I pray that people are convinced of truth each time I preach, not because of the force of my words or the ingenuity of my argument, but by the power of the Holy Spirit. Jesus said, "When the Spirit of truth comes, he will guide you into all the truth; for he will not speak on his own, but will speak whatever he hears, and he will declare to you the things that are to come." (John 16:13). I pray that this is true for the reflections and sermons found in this book.

So take my hand! I invite you to join me through a year at a special church with very special people. From beginning to end, through frustrations and joys, with difficult questions and in tentative answers, I pray that you, dear reader, will honor the truest intention of this book: may you *think* about your faith. To God be the glory forever and ever.

Andrew Taylor-Troutman
New Dublin Presbyterian Church
Dublin, Virginia
September, 2011

1

The New and the Unexpected

DAILY COMMUTES

ONE OF THE BEST perks about my job is the "morning commute." New Dublin Presbyterian Church sits at the end of a private road, elevated on a slight ridge. To get to my office from the manse, I simply walk about three hundred yards underneath ancient oak trees, past an iconic cemetery, and into a little white church with a green metal roof. Farmland stretches for miles all around and the green hills gently slope at the horizon. The landscape is beautiful and tranquil; it makes you want to take a deep breath and be at peace.

I try my best to maintain a welcoming office space at this pictur-esque church. I want the inside of the church to be just as open and inviting to visitors as the surrounding landscape. Despite this goal, I knew from my very first day on the job that much of my time should be spent out of the office. In the eyes of the folk at New Dublin, the work of a pastor is not confined to his or her study. As people come to church, I am expected to visit their homes. We are a throwback to the days when "preacher's cookies" were whipped up on the spot because the preacher had dropped by unannounced for a friendly chat.

I have learned to appreciate these "afternoon commutes" to people's homes just as much as my time in the office. Sometimes we must allow others to welcome us. A pastoral visit is like many social situations in that there is a great deal of importance placed upon food! In my first ten days of visiting alone, I ate ice cream, cookies, banana pudding, brown-ies, and strawberries, not to mention cup after cup of strong, black cof-fee. While I quickly learned that I could not keep track of all the edible gifts I received, I will admit that there have been several occasions when

I have been grateful for the caffeine. The rules of etiquette for pastoral visitation include some tedious formalities. For instance, the summer forecast for southwestern Virginia inevitably includes some chance of thunderstorms, and most of my parishioners seem to enjoy speculating upon this ubiquitous topic. This can make me a little drowsy.

Do not assume, however, that I have been bored by my conversations. I am often amazed by the things people will share. During one visit, a woman described an evening when she looked out of her bedroom window and saw a vision of her brother-in-law dancing across the mountains in the distance. About two hours later, she received a phone call that he had died. Another parishioner is visited each night by a bright light that she believes is an angel. Such conversations are not held around a typical dinner table!

While a pastoral visit may include a discussion about the weather or a detailed chronicling of various aches and pains, I try to be patient and attentive because even the most mundane conversations can lead to a meaningful discussion of faith. Towards the end of the visit, I typically ask, "What have you been praying about lately?" I have seen this question act like a key that unlocks the real struggle inside. Quite unexpectedly, someone may give voice to what lies heavily on the heart.

One day I had an appointment to visit a family, but mistakenly presented myself at the wrong house. Though I was completely unexpected and unannounced, this church member graciously invited me inside. Even early in my ministry, I was beginning to understand the importance of hospitality in this culture. We sat at his kitchen table, drinking cold water from the well and chatting amicably. He and I do not have a great deal of experiences in common, and this fact became even more apparent as we talked. For instance, I do not include feeding the cows as part of my Sunday routine to get ready for church. While I enjoyed our time together, I knew that we both needed to get back to work. Just before I was about to leave for my scheduled appointment, I offered to pray for him and his family.

In response to my request for prayer concerns, tears fell freely down his sun-browned face. I couldn't have been more surprised than if I saw a vision of my sister-in-law dancing across the distant mountains! This steady rock of the church whose clear blue eyes seemed forever set to the task at hand was *crying*. He shared the details of a sudden and tragic loss in the extended family, which had left him with questions about his faith. There in the kitchen, he added his voice to the great chorus of faithful people who have cried out in anguish, "*Why God?*"

I do not know how helpful I was to this parishioner on that day. I did not have much to say in response to his questions, much less any answers. I was still learning to find my way, literally around Dublin and figuratively as a pastor. But I was grateful for this unexpected visit and the chance to listen. Though I had visited the wrong house, sometimes we don't know where we are going until we've already arrived.

This unexpected visit points to another lesson I learned quickly at New Dublin: some mistakes are actually gifts.

My first Sunday in the pulpit was Pentecost, which marks the church's celebration of the gift of the Holy Spirit. According to the book of Acts, this spirit of fire came from heaven with a sound like a mighty rush of wind (Acts 2:2). How ironic that the very first sound out of my mouth was the mighty sound of microphone feedback! Though the sound system's malfunction nearly busted everyone's eardrums, this unexpected event did prove to be an unexpected blessing. As our ears rang, everyone shared a laugh, and I could see the anxiety melting away from their faces. I felt my own apprehension easing off my shoulders.

Perhaps others would have preferred a more somber or professional introduction. As I've reflected about this incident, I think it is a great illustration of the grace that my congregation affords me. I also believe that we could laugh together because we had started to trust each other. My reputation was growing as a "preacher who likes to visit." Even before the first sermon, we were forming relationships that could stand the test of mishaps. This has continued to serve us well to this very day, no matter where life leads us on our daily commutes.

COWS ARE COOL!

While I do value pastoral visitation, I also spend a great deal of time in the church office. I love to study and I love to learn. I want to teach my academic knowledge by putting the wealth of biblical and theological scholarship into the language of the laity. Craig Barnes writes of the importance of "the fresh articulation of familiar old truths in a specific context."[1] The message must be translated so it can be understood in a

---

1. Barnes, *The Pastor as Minor Poet*, 26.

deeply personal way, which Barnes terms as "a realm beneath the presenting issues."[2] We may have daily conversations about the weather, but the Bible and theological tradition speak to our hearts if we can only hear their messages as addressed to us.

As a pastor, serving as such a translator is much easier to understand within the walls of a study than it is to put into practice in the life of the congregation. Rob Bell offers a metaphor for this difficulty as "playing the piano while wearing oven mitts." Bell explains: "We can make a noise, sometimes even hit the notes well enough to bang out a melody, but it doesn't sound like it could, or should. The elements are all there—fingers, keys, strings, ears—but there's something in the way, something inhibiting our ability to fully experience all the possibilities."[3] Bell's image resonates with me. In reviewing sermons for this book, certain messages that I was trying to proclaim were not nearly as clear or as sharp as I would have liked for them to sound. I have cringed in embarrassment at some of the "notes" of my sermons. I take comfort in the fact that, just as there is grace to be found in mistakes, so grace can be heard in any sermon.

Here, then, is yet another importance of pastoral visits: messages can be learned through relationships. By reaching out to people in their physical space, we can discern where others are in their spiritual journey. It is fine and good to make declarative statements about theology and faith, but I've already suggested that it is the right *question* that unlocks a deep meaning in a personal way. By listening attentively and seeking to learn from others, perhaps we will then discover opportunities to translate some of that wonderful scholarship into words that ring true. Moreover, preachers can be taught a great deal by the classroom of daily experience.

On another visit during my first week as a pastor, I had asked a grandmother to tell me a little about her grandson. She responded by telling this story: Her ten-year-old grandson was visiting their farmhouse one evening last winter when his grandfather went out to feed the cattle. Despite his grandmother's urging, the young man declined the invitation to accompany him. He was still watching television, comfortable by the fire, when the grandfather came back inside with a young calf cradled in his arms. This poor animal had fallen in the creek and was nearly

2. Ibid., 19.

3. Bell, *Love Wins*, 61.

frozen to death. Grandpa set the calf down in the living room and began vigorously rubbing its body with warm towels. Forget the television; the grandson was now transfixed by this battle against death. Wordlessly his grandfather held out another towel with his free hand. The boy grabbed it and joined in massaging the calf back to life. Thankfully, this towel therapy worked and that baby calf eventually stumbled to its feet in that awkward way of theirs. Then the grandson willingly accompanied his grandfather to the barn for the chores. In fact, he insisted on tagging along! The child came back and proudly announced, "Cows are cool!"

Imbedded in a grandmother's love for her grandson is a valuable lesson for pastors. In order to preach, we must be in relationship. We must accept the offered towel or outstretched hand, and be willing to work beside the people in our congregation. Just as the boy's insight into cows was gained through the laborious, even potentially tragic work alongside his grandfather, so a sermon must be forged in a loving relationship with parishioners. Even if the message does not hit all the right notes, something of God's truth will be communicated.

To appreciate the deep wisdom of a child's lesson that "cows are cool," I have learned from Wendell Berry that I need to "let the farm judge." A novelist, essayist, and poet, Berry is also a man who shows tremendous appreciation for the art of farming. For instance, he writes of the importance of animal husbandry in light of the needs of the land. Knowledge and skill, including modern breeding practices, play a vital role. But a conscientious farmer should "let the farm judge" which breed is most compatible with environmental factors, such as topography, climate, and soil quality. For instance, Berry's farm is along the lower Kentucky River valley, so he grazes a breed of hill sheep that can maneuver across the landscape and eat the natural vegetation.[4]

Let me be clear that I am not making a pejorative comparison between the congregation of New Dublin and a farm! My point is I am coming into an existing ecosystem that has functioned before me and will continue to do so after I leave. My role is proactive; I am here to "work the land." My tools are exegetical methods to till the fertile soil of the Bible. With prayer and patience, these seeds I plant may blossom and help people think theologically.

But I also feel a deep sense of respect for the parishioners and their ways of learning. The Spirit's gift on Pentecost, after all, was the ability to

4. Berry, "Let the Farm Judge," 51–53

speak in multiple languages. As the Holy Spirit empowered the people, the good news was translated so that others could hear of the mighty acts of God in their own languages (Acts 2:7–8). Just as our daily commutes and routine conversations might take us into unexpected territories and profound moments, so might God speak to us in new ways through our everyday experience. And it seems to me that this is pretty cool.

"NEW BIRDS IN THE TREES"

May 22nd, 2010
Acts 2:1–21

So, here I am—the new pastor on the block and a part of the new family in the manse. Everything that I see and do is *new* to me. For instance, I wake up early to go running around my new neighborhood. Everywhere I look, I see signs of the new day dawning: the rising sun, the dew on the grass, the morning mist. I thank God for each new day because I am excited to be here with you, excited about our new ministry together. Sometimes I swear that the birds roosting in the beautiful old oak trees by the cemetery are actually chirping, "New! New! *New!*"

The more I've thought about all of these new things, however, the more I've realized that even a new day is also part of an old pattern. The sun rises and sets. The next day it rises again, only to go back down the next evening. It is true that each morning is the start of a new day; but it is also true that even new things are still part of a larger history.

Over the years there have been many new people here at New Dublin Presbyterian Church, including many pastors. All of these generations of people remain a part of our new ministry because they are a part of us today. This is like the fact that my maternal grandfather passed away over fifteen years ago, but I still wear my watch upside down just like he did. I can look at a complete stranger smoking a pipe and vividly remember him. When I sling my arm over the back of a chair, my mother says that I remind her of him. Today she is watching me do new things in front of my new church, but Granddad is somehow here as well. Who we are today is shaped in part by those who came before us. The past is also present.

After only one week, I've already witnessed the past becoming present when you share your stories with me. Different parts of your history can be funny or serious, hopeful or sad. But no matter what, these stories are a part of you, and I am eager to listen. As your new pastor, I want to understand how the church has shaped your life. Getting to know you includes learning where you've been and who you've been with.

How fitting, then, that today we celebrate the start of our new ministry while we mark the beginning of the church at Pentecost. In our scripture from Acts, we remember that the gift of the Holy Spirit came from heaven like a rushing wind and appeared like tongues of fire. Suddenly Galileans could speak languages from all corners of the world. Things were new, new, *new*!

But notice that Peter explains these new things to the crowd in Jerusalem by citing the *Old* Testament. He quotes the prophet Joel, who wrote centuries before him about the outpouring of the Spirit (Acts 2:14–21). Peter spoke of new events, yet he emphasized that these events were also part of a history. At Pentecost, the past was also present.

By this point in my first sermon, I expect that some of you are thinking, "Amen!" Have you been worried that this new pastor was going to come into your church with a head too full of new ideas to listen to your cherished past?

I know a story about a young Methodist preacher who arrived at his new church fresh out of seminary. Immediately he noticed a certain tree in the front of the sanctuary. In fact, he bemoaned the fact that the tree was ugly and so very *old*. Not only was it an eyesore, the tree was leaning against the building and damaging the roof. This young preacher decided to fix this problem once and for all: he decided to cut the tree down.

Less than a day later, that same pastor was on his way out of town *never* to return! Why did the church dismiss him so quickly? He had cut down the tree planted by John Wesley, the famous founder of the Methodist church! In his eagerness to do something new, that pastor had destroyed the Wesley oak, that church's oldest and most beloved possession.

Since New Dublin Presbyterian Church has been around even longer than John Wesley, I'm sure that this congregation has its own versions of the Wesley oak. You can rest assured that I am *not* going to cut them down. In fact, I honor the proud history of this congregation and believe in the legacy built by faithful generations. The past is present and should be honored.

Yet the past should not be worshipped. On Pentecost, Peter remembered the history of Israel's prophets, but then he spoke of a new reality. Peter proclaimed the *power* of the Holy Spirit: the mighty, rushing wind that brought so many different people together. While I don't believe that we should cut down the Wesley oak, Pentecost must not only be a celebration of the church's past. I believe that the same power that inspired those first disciples wants to empower our church in new ways.

Perhaps some of you are hesitant to say, "Amen," to this last idea. I am aware of a saying that some Christians want the Spirit to be like airplane coffee: weak, reliable, and given in small amounts. In the book of Acts, however, the Holy Spirit can hardly be compared to airplane coffee. In fact, the actions of the Spirit are often hard for the early Christians to swallow. The Spirit blesses both Jews and Gentiles; the Spirit starts new congregations in different parts of the world; the Spirit ordains both men and women to positions of leadership despite the fact that they do not exactly have the best resumes.

As your new pastor, I have already seen signs that the Spirit is moving in our midst, inspiring new things all around us. New youth are playing our organ. New leaders are working with our youth group. There is a new women's fellowship. There is a new fundraiser to dig new wells in Africa. There are new plans to reinvigorate our partnership with a church in Mexico. The Holy Spirit inspires new ideas and encourages new activities. Over the next couple of months, you may hear the birds around here and swear that they are chirping, "New! New! *New!*"

As your new pastor, I would only ask that you join me in asking for the Spirit's guidance. Let us pray to strike a balance between the old and the new. Let us pray for the power of the Holy Spirit to bring new life *and* maintain tradition. Let us pray for the wisdom to move forward with the past still present. By the power of the Holy Spirit, may *new* birds roost in the beautiful old trees, and may every member at New Dublin hear their songs of praise.

2

Open Eyes, Open Table

THE TABLE RUNNETH OVER

WHILE PEOPLE IN RURAL Appalachia rarely sing their own praises, the members of New Dublin do take a great deal of pride in their hospitality. They love to tell the story of an interim moderator who served before I arrived. Apparently, this pastor wanted our session to come to his church and show his members how to put on a potluck supper. Ginny and I learned about the New Dublin expertise in this area almost immediately. Before we were even settled into the manse, there was a potluck held in our honor.

Stepping into the fellowship hall that evening, I took in the scene with a sweeping glance. My gaze was drawn to the table in the middle of the room. It was clean and simple, draped neatly with a white cloth and adorned with a small, colorful arrangement of wildflowers. This table seemed to hold great promise of things to come. As the church members arrived, covered dishes piled up around the flower centerpiece: salads, deviled eggs, pastas, breads, and all manner of meats and vegetables. The table became a heavy-laden cornucopia of bright colors.

Likewise, my mind began to fill up with knowledge of the parishioners. I met one member who had adopted four children from Central America and then met one of her grandchildren, drooling happily in a stroller. I hugged a teary-eyed matriarch of the congregation who recently lost her husband. I squatted down to high-five young children and leaned over to hug people in wheelchairs. I discovered that there were multiple men named Jim and several women named Diane. To avoid confusion, a retired professor from a local university graciously gave me photographs of most of the members with their names written on the back. With a knowing nod, Bernadine explained to me that she learned the names of her students with this method. With such thoughtful and kind actions, I felt a deep sense of confirmation. In smile after smile, hug after hug, I felt that this is the place I am supposed to be. At one point, I looked over at Ginny. Through the half circle of chattering people that had formed around her, she smiled and I hoped that she felt the same way.

When the table was finally full with food, everyone in the room turned expectantly towards me. I took a deep breath. Anticipating this moment, I had planned exactly what I wanted to say ahead of time. But I had not foreseen the incredible hospitality of this reception. I was so touched that I abandoned my memorized script, and, quoting from Psalm 23, simply said that "my cup runneth over." That phrase from the King James Bible was the best way I knew to speak to the wonderful sense of abundance at that table and with these people. That potluck was a holy communion for me, a sacred gathering of food and fellowship that embodied generosity and hospitality.

MY FIRST COMMUNION

In many traditions, the idea of "first communion" refers to the first time one receives the sacrament. This celebration usually takes place after a period of instruction like confirmation or catechism. I am using the designation in this chapter to refer to the first time I officiated the sacrament because my first communion likewise represents the culmination of theological training. It was truly an important step for me, just as meaningful as my first sermon. After all, I was ordained to be a minister of word *and* sacrament.

Although presiding at the Lord's Table was the result of years of study and preparation, I think of my first communion as a starting point rather than an end goal. This also relates to my ordination: I am called to serve these people in this place. Just as I felt a strong sense of confirmation at the welcoming potluck, I believe that the congregation's perception of me changed after my first communion. I think I became less of the "new pastor" and more of "our pastor." Paradoxically, this shift may well have occurred because of unplanned events rather than my diligent preparations.

In the days leading up to my first communion, we forgot to appoint elders to serve. Not only that, but an hour before the service, we realized that we did not have grape juice! Thankfully, certain elders had arrived early, and they were calmer than their frazzled pastor. Someone went out and bought the grape juice. Another filled the communion trays with bread and then the communion cups with juice. Three others volunteered to be servers. Thanks to their quick and decisive actions, all of the elements were in place about fifteen minutes before the service.

The elders gathered around the Lord's Table and listened kindly as I nervously instructed them about the logistics of a ritual that they already knew how to perform. I had practiced for hours in the days before my first communion. I wanted to reciprocate the hospitality that I received at that New Dublin table during the potluck by presiding at the Lord's Table with grace and dignity. So I had memorized all the various parts of the liturgy.

Without any notes, I got off to a great start. I remembered each line of the responsive prayers. I broke the bread and poured the cup with great flourish. After the elders distributed the bread and the cups, I collected their trays like a veteran, neatly stacked them, and launched into the prayer after communion. Despite my gusto for this prayer, I do remembering having an uneasy feeling that something was wrong.

One of the elders interrupted my prayer by whispering urgently, "Andrew. Andrew. *Andrew*!" When he finally had my attention, he pointed, first to himself, and then down towards the rest of pew to the servers who sat with puzzled looks. Then it dawned on me that I had forgotten to serve the servers! I was able to suspend the prayer abruptly and distribute the elements. Though embarrassed, I was grateful for the elder's timely interruption. While the liturgy did not flow as smoothly as I had rehearsed all week, I would have deeply regretted leaving anyone out of the Lord's Supper.

After the service, most people made passing references to my mistake with gentle amusement in their eyes. I was happy to laugh with them. In reference to that memorable beginning of my first Sunday, we joked that at least my microphone had worked correctly. I think that people appreciate the fact that I am not easily ruffled and can make the best out of my slip-ups. Perhaps such blunders are endearing because they show a human side of a pastor. Over the course of my first year, I heard several approving comments relating to the fact that I am not "too big for my britches." This culture values modesty.

On a deeper level, I had just preached a sermon about hospitality as a spiritual discipline. Just before I forgot to serve the elders, the body of Christ celebrated our belief that Jesus is the Great Host. Since our risen Lord invites us to his table solely by grace, we ate and drank together as sinners—as people who make mistakes. If this is part of the human condition, then maybe such "mistakes" are really more like opportunities to practice the kind of hospitality that Jesus practiced. Maybe we are modeling for one another the belief that there is nothing that can prevent us from coming to the Lord's Table—nothing that we could do, or not do, to forfeit our savior's gracious invitation.

Holy Communion is ultimately about the grace of God. We refer to the *Lord's* Table, not Andrew's table nor New Dublin's table nor even the Presbyterians' table. It does not matter if you practiced all week to get the Words of Institution exactly right but flubbed the liturgy or if you came late to church and forgot to bring the grape juice. If the point is that we are all invited, then we witness to this hospitality by welcoming one another. We extend grace to others because Jesus first extended grace to us.

I take a great deal of comfort in the message of grace found at the Lord's Table. Yet there is a scandalous aspect to practicing radical hospitality in Jesus' name. It is one thing to talk about worshipping together despite our silly mistakes. But what about the wife whose husband is cheating on her? Is he still invited? Is each spouse involved in this gut-wrenching and heart-breaking situation invited to the *same* table? What about families that have been torn apart over inheritances? Are both sides of the dispute, even if one is clearly at fault, invited to eat the *same* bread and drink of the *same* cup? Such questions provide a challenge for us to live as the body of Christ, even as we break bread in remembrance of him.

Jesus once told a parable about an older brother who was fuming mad because his father threw a grandiose feast for his younger brother. This prodigal son had made many mistakes in a land far away. By his own estimation, he was not worthy to be considered a member of the family, much less the reason for festivity. That was certainly the opinion of the older brother. Still the father throws a celebration for this prodigal and then goes to his other son who was bitterly angry out in the cold fringes of the party's light. The father lovingly said, "We had to celebrate and rejoice, because this brother of yours was dead and has come to life; he was lost and has been found" (Luke 15:32).

It is striking to me that Jesus ends his parable with these words. What a scandal he places before us! Since the elder brother does not respond to his father, the same question falls into our laps. How might we witness to such grace in our communities today?

For my first communion service, I borrowed an idea from one of my seminary professors, Paul Galbreath. I encouraged the congregation to pray the Great Thanksgiving liturgy with their eyes *open*.[1] When I prayed from the Lord's Table, I was able to lock eyes with them. In the exact moments of my first communion prayer, I was mostly in my own head, thinking about the words I had memorized and so carefully practiced ahead of time. As I have reflected on the experience, however, several faces have come to mind: the smile on her face, the tears running down his cheeks, and the look of pride in my parents' eyes. I treasure these memories of those different faces as snapshots of the scandalous yet beautiful belief that Jesus invites us all to the same table no matter what we are feeling or have experienced beforehand.

In the following weeks, the snapshots of those faces during the prayer became living portraits of people's lives. I learned that many people received some kind of "first communion" on that Sunday. They ate the bread for the first time without a spouse or for the first time as an expectant mother. They drank from the cup for the first time as an unemployed father or for the first time as a homeowner. Yet no matter what we have done or what has happened to us, the elements of this meal are always the same. With our open eyes fixed on our Lord's Table, we can see evidence of God's unchanging love in the breaking of bread and the pouring of the cup. Like the father of Jesus' famous parable, God "sees" us no matter how far off we have traveled and invites us to the feast (Luke 15:20). For all of the "first-timers" who come to the Lord's Table, I pray that they will look to these constants to provide a sense of comfort.

Our open eyes can help us with the scandal of grace as well. Like the older brother, we are confronted and challenged by God's hospitality. In light of what God has done for us, we can learn to see one another other as members of the same family of faith despite our mistakes, errors, and sins. As we pray with our eyes open, we are inspired to practice

1. Galbreath, *Leading from the Table*, 109–110.

hospitality. Since we eat at the same table, we should take the time and invest the energy to help during the transitions of the all "firsts" and "lasts" in our lives.

I preached about hospitality that Sunday morning when I served communion for the first time, but I learned about hospitality when I brought communion into homes during the following week. I discovered that hospitality is about sharing strawberries and iced tea before the breaking of the bread and pouring of the cup. When sharing home communion, I found out that there is a great deal of laughter beforehand and sometimes there are tears afterwards. As a result, my prayers are less formal and more personal in someone's home.

I had to abandon my well-rehearsed communion script in other ways as well. The personal experience of home communion naturally leads to personal exchanges between the pastor and those who receive the sacrament. For instance, one gentleman abruptly interrupted the liturgical prayer to ask about my wife's new job. On a different occasion, a matriarch of our congregation repeated the Lord's Prayer with me, but then kept right on going after the "amen," adding words of thanksgiving for the people of her beloved church. Often a parishioner spills grape juice down his or her shirt while struggling to drink from those tiny glasses. I break off smaller pieces of bread so that the elderly communicant will not accidentally choke, and sometimes I place the food directly in his or her mouth. Thank God for all of these improvisations! Our sacrament does not take place in a vacuum apart from shaky hands and short attention spans, just as the body of Christ cannot be contained by the four walls of a particular church. Neither is the difference between pastor and parishioner so rigidly defined as it can appear to be during the celebration of a sacrament in Sunday worship. All of us are sharing real bread, real juice, and real fellowship together. Whenever and wherever we partake of Holy Communion, the point is that God will be real to us.

In the beautiful text about the journey to Emmaus, the two travelers cannot recognize Jesus on their own (Luke 24:15–16). God must come to us in order to be revealed. Grace is the first cause; and yet there is a task for us. We are to practice hospitality by insisting that even strangers join us around our tables (Luke 24:29). Because God first invited us, we must go to people who cannot come to us. As it was in the breaking of the bread that the companions recognized Jesus, so must we recognize the image of God in each other through sharing the sacrament. In the same Emmaus story, Jesus immediately vanishes after he is recognized (Luke 24:31). It seems to me that we need to continue the practice of breaking bread together in order to see him again. Then we might see our tables at home and at church running over with the abundance of grace.

"TASTE AND SEE"

July 4th, 2010
Luke 10:1–12, 17–20

A discipline is a habit or a training that results in a certain pattern of behavior. If someone were to ask us to compile a list of spiritual disciplines, we would think of activities that are designed to make us faithful Christians. I imagine that we would start with prayer and Bible study. Then we might add regular church attendance, tithing, and fasting. These are well known spiritual disciplines. What about the practice of hospitality? Would that make our list?

Perhaps we don't usually think of hosting a traveler for dinner as a pattern of Christian behavior; maybe we don't even think about church potlucks in a spiritual sense. Yet we should adjust our thinking.

Hospitality might not have been the first idea that struck you about this morning's text. But when Jesus sends out the seventy into the mission field, he invites them to experience the hospitality of others. Jesus instructed these missionaries to remain in the homes that welcomed them, eating and drinking whatever was provided (Luke 10:7). While the missionaries are important, Jesus declares the importance of their hosts as well. The mission of the seventy would not have worked without the generous hospitality of these strangers.

There are also other texts in the Bible that point to the importance of hospitality. Consider the story of Abraham and three unexpected guests who turned out to be angels (Gen 18:1–15). The moral of this account is, "Do not neglect to show hospitality to strangers, for by doing that some have entertained angels without knowing it" (Heb 13:2). As the biblical word for "angel" can be translated as "messenger," hosting a messenger of Jesus is the practice of entertaining angels.

Hospitality, then, is a *spiritual* discipline. One of my former professors, Paul Galbreath, has written that hospitality is the practice of meeting with friends or strangers so that we can meet God.[2] We share a meal and share a laugh; we open our homes and open our hearts; and we discover Emmanuel—God with us.

Today we have the opportunity to practice hospitality by celebrating Holy Communion. The Lord's Supper is a commemoration of the Last Supper between Jesus and his disciples during the Jewish Passover. As Jesus *hosted* this meal to symbolize his sacrifice for those seated around his table, our observance of Holy Communion is a celebration of Jesus as the Great Host. Jesus pulls out a chair and invites each one of us to sit down. Grace is the only word to describe such an invitation. God invites us, not because of anything that we have accomplished or merited, but because of what God has done in the death and resurrection of Jesus Christ. This is the divine practice of hospitality.

But our Great Host gives us a responsibility as well. Whenever we eat this bread and drink this wine, we are reminded of Jesus' words on the night he was betrayed: *do this in remembrance of me.* The importance of "doing this" is reflected in the spiritual discipline of hospitality. Communion is not just about our individual relationship with God; instead we are commanded by the remembrance of our Lord to welcome one another, to share food and drink, and to pray together. Just as the mission of the seventy was made possible by the hospitality of strangers, so our acts of welcome can have a profound impact upon others.

Journalist Sara Miles was an atheist. One day, for no apparent reason, she happened to walk into a service and receive communion for the first time. She had never been to this particular church before, yet she was invited to receive the sacrament. What happened next was nothing less than miraculous; in her words, "Jesus happened to me."[3]

Her personal experience of Jesus was so profound that Miles converted to Christianity and began to worship regularly at that church. But the story does not end there; something equally as miraculous as her experience of Christ occurred when she started practicing hospitality as a spiritual discipline. She writes, "What happened once I started

2. Ibid., 56–57.
3. Miles, *Take This Bread*, 58.

distributing communion was the truly disturbing, dreadful realization about Christianity: you can't be a Christian by yourself."[4]

After this dramatic revelation, Miles started a food pantry to feed the homeless. Her ministry grew until her food pantries fed more than a thousand families every week! How does she explain such an amazing ministry? She wrote in her memoir, "It was about action. Taste and see, the Bible said, and I did. My first, questioning year at church ended with a question whose urgency would propel me into work I'd never imagined: now that you've taken the bread, what are you going to do?"[5]

As we celebrate the transformative power of Holy Communion in our lives, I want to take this question to heart. Miles' emphasized that her experience at the Lord's Table was about action: taste and see! Communion is an *eye-opening* experience.

This morning, I invite us to see hospitality as a spiritual discipline. I challenge us to receive communion as a life-altering experience. In just a moment, I invite you to pray the Communion Prayer of Thanksgiving with your eyes *open*.[6]

By keeping our eyes open, we see the bread being broken and the cup being poured. By keeping our eyes open, we see the people around us. We are reminded that the Lord is our Great Host and that we are called to be hosts for one another. We remember God's grace that invites us to the table and to serve in our communities.

This table is the Lord's Table and it is wide open to anyone who would take the bread and the cup. So then, may we come with our eyes wide open, remembering Jesus our Great Host, and staring grace directly in the faces of one another. My friends, taste and *see* that the Lord is good.

4. Ibid., 96.

5. Ibid., 97.

6. Galbreath, *Leading from the Table*, 109–110.

3

Take My Hand

PRACTICING SELF-CARE

M Y BROTHER, JOHN, AND his wife, Kelly, came to visit shortly after I arrived in the town of Dublin. They live in Brooklyn, which is a long way from my home in more ways than one. Kelly remarked that it was amazing to hear the crickets at night instead of the traffic. Her comment took me by surprise; I had been thinking about next week's sermon. My mind was as busy and congested as a street in Manhattan. After only a few weeks on the job, I realized that I needed to take better care of myself.

Sabbath is a time of rest and renewal. It is also one of the Ten Commandments (Exod 20:8–11; Deut 5:12–15). While no sermon would suggest that the other nine laws are optional, even the best pastors sometimes act as if honoring the Sabbath was merely a friendly suggestion. When Barbara Brown Taylor worked in the parish, she stayed just as busy on her "day off" as any other day. With refreshing candor, she examines her inability to rest: "Taking a full day off was so inconceivable that I made up reasons why it was not possible. If stopped for a whole day, there would be no more weekend weddings . . . Sick people would languish in the hospital and begin to question their faith. Parishioners would start a rumor that I was not a real shepherd but only a hired hand . . . If I stopped for a whole day, God would be sorely disappointed in me."[1]

It is due to such anxiety that Stanley Hauerwas refers to most Protestant pastors as quivering masses of availability. I am aware that

1. Taylor, *Leaving Church*, 135.

I often bend over backwards to please people, rather than make any effort to take care of myself. The desire to be needed often trumps the desire to relax. Like Taylor, I don't want a poor reputation among my parishioners. I don't want to miss an opportunity for ministry. Perhaps on a deeper level, I don't want God to be disappointed in me either. On the very first night of my first vacation as a pastor, I dreamed that one of my parishioners had just lost her mother in a tragic accident. I knew full well that this person's mother has been dead for years. In my dream, however, she had died suddenly and everyone was waiting for me at the funeral. What a nightmare!

In my conscious mind, I know that Sabbath-keeping is not a luxury. Not only was it mandated in the Ten Commandments, the first creation story beautifully illustrates that rest was part of the original divine intention (Gen 2:1–3). Following a long tradition of Jewish interpreters, Jesus maintained that the practice was for our health and well-being: "The Sabbath was made for humankind, and not humankind for the Sabbath" (Mark 2:27). Scripture teaches that God is not "disappointed" with those who honor the spiritual practice of renewal and refreshment.

When I had that nightmare about the funeral, my family was in Scotland for my father's first sabbatical after twenty-five years of ministry. This was an amazing opportunity, and I tried to relax. From a train window, I looked over the landscape of northwestern Scotland and noticed a great similarity to southwestern Virginia. Just like back home, I saw purple wildflowers, red farmhouses, gray distant mountains, and green rolling hills. Yet not everything was the same: because Scotland is farther north, the climate is colder and the growing season is later. While grain was still growing in their fields, the hay was cut and baled back in Dublin. I have come to think of this difference as a fitting metaphor for the Sabbath. My time away is not the time for harvesting; the work I was called to do at New Dublin is finished like the baled hay. This realization has continued to help me relax, even long after my family came back and I returned to work.

I've also tried to honor the Sabbath as part of my worship of God. In retrospect, Taylor learned a profound spiritual reason, not simply to take a day off, but to obey the Sabbath commandment: "The clear promise is that those who rest like God find themselves free like God, no longer slaves to the thousand compulsions that send others rushing towards their graves."[2] No longer quivering masses of availability, we are free to serve others out of love. I once told my wife that I would stop at nothing until I had led her to happiness. I was referring to my new position as a pastor and about how I was going to make everything perfect in Dublin for us. Ginny replied, "Take my hand, and we'll find our way together."

As we are all on a journey through life, I have come to believe that we need the support of other people in order to keep the Sabbath.

SABBATH FOR US

There is an Amish community less than thirty miles from New Dublin Presbyterian Church. Since some of my parishioners live in this area, I have a unique window and fascinating insight into the Amish lifestyle.

First of all, the Amish take the Sabbath seriously. Very seriously. On Sunday, their businesses are closed, only the most basic chores are completed, and everyone goes to worship. At first glance, their community seems to be in perfect harmony with the rhythms of work and rest. But the Amish lifestyle does not mean peace for everyone.

The Amish straddle a fine line with their non-Amish neighbors, referred to as "the English." While they are intentional about restricting outside influence upon their way of life, the Amish impact the lives of others, especially in a small community. Some of these influences are minor inconveniences, such as horse manure on the roads. Others, however, are quite jarring. Though the Amish do not drive gasoline-powered vehicles, they do hire huge trucks and other pieces of large equipment to build their homes, farms, and businesses. I spoke with one "English" neighbor who bitterly complained that the Amish have inundated their peaceful community with a barrage of loud machinery. Now there is something I never expected to hear.

Despite my initial impression about their practice of the Sabbath, the Amish are not even at peace among themselves. Shortly before I arrived to the area, their community split over a theological issue. There was a charismatic movement among a few families who demanded to be re-baptized by immersion. The more traditional Amish balked, so some families "jumped the fence" and are no longer part of the community.

Let me be clear that I admire and respect much about the Amish. Rather than criticize their lifestyle, my point is that even a strict adher-

2. Ibid., 136.

ence to the Sabbath does not necessarily translate to peace and harmony. Furthermore, I certainly do not wish to appear overly critical of others because there is a great deal of tension and the potential for schism in my own tradition.

During my first summer at New Dublin, the Presbyterian Church of the United States of America was embroiled yet again in the controversy over the ordination of gay, lesbian, bisexual, and transgender people. Our general assembly passed an amendment to the ordination standards, which meant that the proposal was sent to the presbyteries. This process is roughly analogous to the United States Congress approving an amendment to the Constitution and needing ratification from the states. In the PC (USA), Amendment 10A passed in 2011.

The goal of the amendment, as I understand it, was actually to make the standards for ordination more reflective of a person's total commitment to the faith. The language of Amendment 10A required each person to "submit joyfully to the Lordship of Jesus Christ" as part of the requirements of ordination. I find it ironic that many of those against this change would fully support such a statement in other contexts. In this case, opposition arose because the new language replaced the ordination standard known as the "fidelity and chastity" clause, which mandated fidelity in marriage and chastity in singleness. Since marriage is defined exclusively between a man and a woman, this clause effectively barred people in same gender relationships from ordination.

For me, this national debate was deeply personal; several of my dearest friends could not serve the church they love with their talents, hearts, and minds because of the gender of the person whom they loved. I support Amendment 10A so that all may serve who are gifted by God for ordained ministry. Though I realize the debate is divisive, it is my opinion that ultimately our church will become stronger, larger, and more faithful because of the gifted individuals who are now able to serve alongside us.

Opinions about this amendment vary at New Dublin. We have both card-carrying Republicans and bumper sticker Democrats. Though I am to the left of the majority of my parishioners on the issue of homosexual ordination, I try to be respectful to every single person. For many on both sides, this issue hits close to home. Regardless of one's opinion about an amendment, always remember that an issue may have a face, and that face may be a loved one.

While everyone is not going to agree, we can strive for unity—we can continue to worship and work together in ministry. New Dublin understands this better than most churches I've encountered. It seems to me that our ability to live together, despite our differences of opinion, is related to our practice of Sabbath.

During the spring and fall, New Dublin Presbyterian Church makes time for "lemonade on the lawn." Immediately after worship, we gather under the canopy of oak trees outside of the sanctuary. Perhaps we have other places to be; maybe we have important responsibilities elsewhere. But we stop, at least for a moment, and we drink lemonade, eat cookies, and talk to each other. People who disagree on any number of issues still shake hands.

Before our country church is hopelessly stereotyped, I must maintain that our parishioners are just as busy as anyone else in our community. In fact, we seem to get busier all the time. While I was active in sports as a child, it is routine for today's youth to practice a musical instrument, attend an after-school meeting, and play a sports game on the *same* day. When I was growing up in North Carolina, we did not even have practice or rehearsal on Sundays. Today's games start at the 11 o'clock worship hour. I hear parents talk about their dizzying schedules between work, school, errands, and other commitments. While there are benefits to each one of these activities, I think we can safely say that our society is not promoting the practice of Sabbath.

I also believe that there is a connection to be found between the lack of Sabbath-keeping and the increasing level of hostility in our society. There is so little time to stop and think. Little wonder, then, that the nuances of ethical issues rarely sink in. Our political polarization is the equivalent of the microwave meal: pre-packed and half-baked. Our public discourse consists of sound bites that we catch on the way to the next event. We have lost the ability to listen deeply because we are rushing out of the door with the car keys in one hand and the cell phone in the other.

Perhaps part of the solution to bitter partisanship is quite refreshingly simple. New Dublin Presbyterian cannot solve our country's problems, but at the very least, we make time for lemonade on the lawn.

As the pastor, I admit that I work during this Sabbath time. I use lemonade on the lawn as an opportunity to hear about a family member in the hospital, get an update on a child away at school, and meet that neighbor whose been wanting to come to church. I can answer a question about the sermon or offer a personal prayer. In other words, lemonade on the lawn helps me with my job.

But as a Christian, I am incredibly grateful to be a part of a community that models a practice of Sabbath. We are journeying together and should make time to listen to one another. As a church, we need take each other by the hand . . . perhaps now more than ever.

"GOOD INNKEEPERS"

July 11, 2010
Luke 10:25–37

Jesus told a parable about a Samaritan who helped a person lying on the side of the road. The moral is to "go and do likewise" (Luke 10:37). There are thousands of poignant and beautiful stories of people throughout the centuries who helped victimized people. Many good sermons have re-told one of these stories as a means of inspiring people to do the same.

But I imagine that everyone here this morning already has an idea of what it means to be a Good Samaritan. I would guess that many of you have your own personal examples when you or someone you know helped someone else in need.

So this sermon is going to try a new approach by focusing on a different character: the innkeeper. This morning, I'd like for us to put ourselves into the innkeeper's shoes. We know what it means to be a Good Samaritan. What about the Good Innkeeper?

Jesus introduces the innkeeper rather late in the parable. The poor man has already been robbed and beaten; the priest and Levite have come and gone. The Samaritan has stopped and bandaged the man's wounds. Almost at the very end of the story, the Samaritan took the injured man to the inn. Many of us, however, don't follow the story this far. By this point, we have identified with one of the other characters, either positively with the Samaritan or negatively with those who passed by on the other side of the road. But there are others ways for us to identify with the parable; after all, there is another character.

Focusing on the role of the innkeeper in the parable helps me to identify with him. Notice that the innkeeper was asked to help in his usual place of employment; the Good Samaritan brought the man to the inn. He also gave money, so the innkeeper was trusted to be honest with his services. In addition, the innkeeper was asked to go beyond his normal duties and care for the beaten man. The Samaritan left him in charge; he trusts the innkeeper to nurse the beaten man back to health. So the extraordinary actions of the Samaritan also demanded a great deal from the innkeeper. The innkeeper did not choose to help the man lying on the side of the road, but, because he happened to be where he was, the innkeeper was charged to go the extra mile for someone in need. Can you relate to these experiences?

Putting ourselves in the shoes of a character in a parable has a long history of interpretation. For instance, the ancient church leaders read the parable as an analogy, meaning that each character symbolized someone in the real world. Our Vacation Bible School is going to study the parable of the Sower this week. As Jesus explains, the seed represents the word of God and the good soil symbolizes the people who hear God's word.

But many biblical interpreters of the past also read the parable of the Good Samaritan as an analogy. The inn represents the church. Like the inn, the church is a place where people come to be healed. Jesus is the Good Samaritan who rescues people and then brings them to the church. That means that we are like the innkeeper. We have been trusted to continue the ministry of compassion that Jesus began.

This interpretation fascinates me.

Now this familiar parable takes on a whole new meaning! If we identify with the innkeeper, we realize that sometimes the opportunity to help others comes to us. We are called to practice acts of compassion in our everyday jobs. The example of the innkeeper also teaches us that it takes more than one person to lend a helping hand. It seems to me that these are important points to bear in mind.

Often we think of this parable and imagine ourselves as the Good Samaritan. Typically, we are encouraged to stop and assist a person in a car accident on side of the road. It is a good thing to lend a helping hand, but the truth of the matter is that every situation is not a choice between stopping or passing by on the other side. This idea is too simple to ring true in our complex world. From the homeless veteran sitting at the intersection to the media coverage of disasters all over the world, we see and hear of people in need on a daily basis. I don't know about you, but I can feel overwhelmed; I can feel bombarded. If I am always identifying with the Good Samaritan, I feel *helpless*. How can one person meet so many needs? How can I stop for every single person on the side of the road?

I can't; you can't.

But Jesus calls us to go and do likewise! What then can we do?

Instead of comparing every situation to the Good Samaritan, it is helpful to think of ourselves as a community. The church really is like an inn. People come here to find rest and strength for their journey. During their stay, they meet fellow travelers. Even if you have walked a great distance by yourself, you are part of a community once you step foot into the inn. As a group of helpers, we can use our resources to address needs. Like the innkeeper, we are called to be good stewards of financial resources. We are trusted to spend our money and our time in ways that provide care.

When I was interviewing to be the pastor of New Dublin, certain members on the search committee expressed great excitement about a past partnership with a Presbyterian church in Merida, Mexico. I was told that strong relationships have been formed between families and individuals. I was very excited to see this for myself. During my first trip to their church, it was truly wonderful to see the joyful reunions between the Americans and the Mexicans. As people embraced, there was genuine love in everyone's eyes. We visited people in their homes and our brothers and sisters graciously hosted us. Through "Spanglish" and hand gestures, we exchanged details about family members and gave updates about church programs. We rekindled our partnership.

One evening, our group met with their session about ways that we could strengthen the relationship between the two churches. By the end of the meeting, we had agreed to form an email prayer chain to maintain open lines of communication. I was grateful for the commitment to mutuality. This is not a charity project, but an ongoing and evolving partnership, which entails learning and sharing from both parties. This is not a case where we are the Good Samaritans; with our partners in Mexico, we are called to be part of the same inn.

In calling the church to be the hands and feet of the savior, God has charged us to continue the ministry of compassion by working as one community. May we be servants to those Christ calls into our midst; may we be found faithful when Christ comes again to see that those entrusted to our care are nursed back to health; may we all be good innkeepers together.

4

Praying the Questions

THE MYSTERY

ADMITTEDLY, MY PRAYER LIFE has been inconsistent over the course of my life. When I was young, there were many days when I would wake up early just so that I could read my Bible. In the margins, I would scribble little prayers that were prompted by the particular text. I still have that Bible and I like to re-read those prayers, which are snapshots of my faith and my life from years gone by. The prayers are unsophisticated, but I try to be gentle with myself. More often than not, my intensity is evident; it is clear to me, even in looking back, that I was trying to be the best Christian that I possibly could. My dad likes to quote a line from the mystic, Kabir, when describing that time in my life: I was a slave to intensity.[1]

Years later, I think that I was motivated at least in part by a kind of bargaining with God. I was trying to earn blessings by my good behavior. While the blessings that I desired were quite juvenile, I remember thinking that if I did this or if I didn't do that, God would give me exactly what I wanted. This attitude towards prayer lasted well into my adolescence. During my junior year of high school baseball, I was in a deep slump at the plate. I wasn't even hitting the ball out of the infield. One game, I made a big demonstration of prayer, stopping to take a knee and bow my head as I approached the batter's box. I still struck out!

As a pastor, I have encountered in other adults a similar view of a prayer as a bargaining session with God. There seems to be a kind of theology in which it is believed that the prayer will only be efficacious

---

1. Kabir, "The Time Before Death," 53–54.

if the person is fervent enough or pious enough or any number of fill-in-the-blanks. Many people pray before stepping up to the plate, so to speak, and while it certainly seems natural to pray for oneself, the problem is that such attitudes towards prayer can imply a view of God as one who needs to be coerced, convinced, or cajoled. I think we need to think hard about the ramifications of such theology. In the verse just before he teaches the Lord's Prayer, Jesus states emphatically, "Your Father already knows what you need before you ask Him" (Matt 6:8). This makes sense to me. Isn't this part of what we mean by claiming that God is omniscient or all-knowing?

Perhaps what's really going on is a kind of "magical" understanding of prayer. I understand "religious" belief as an idea about the Being (or beings) that are somehow beyond and greater than the human self. "Magical" beliefs would then be the attempt to manipulate those beings. For instance, I know another pastor who once told me that he had prayed away a rain storm. I looked at him in disbelief, not because he would pray for good weather, but because of the magical power that he assigned to his own prayers and, as a consequence, to himself. To put it another way, if prayer is magical, then is God omnipotent or all-powerful?

One thing is for certain: I am expected to pray with people as a pastor. This expectation goes far beyond Sunday morning worship, and rightly so. Faith spills out from the walls of the church, running into homes and hospitals, and even filling up baseball stadiums. I pray for people every day, and I am sincere about those prayers. But I do think that there is a danger that such expectations to pray in different places for different things could go to one's head. (I might start believing that I can control the weather!) Though I recognize my role as a spiritual leader, I consciously resist the implication that my prayers are somehow more powerful than others. When people come to my office for prayer, I often point at the phone on my desk, insisting that is a regular phone and *not* a direct line to God! When asked by the farmers in my congregation to pray for rain, I printed a prayer in the bulletin and encouraged everyone to pray. I tried to stress that this rain prayer was not some kind of magic chant: it is something that we do together.

Yet the question persists, why should we pray? I'm told that Philip Yancey answers that question quite simply: we should pray because Jesus told us to do so. Fine answer! But more to the heart of the matter, what do our prayers do? How does prayer work? Imbedded in these questions is an understanding of the nature of God. Do our prayers have an effect upon God? Does prayer change God's mind or will or plan? Can we pray away a thunderstorm?

Reformed theology responds to these questions by stressing the sovereignty of God. God is in charge; the ruler of all creation has decreed a plan for humankind from the beginning of time, even from before time existed. Prayer, then, cannot be "magical" because we cannot control or compel God. John Calvin rightly warned against praying as if we had the ability to take something from God.[2] We believe that God is both omniscient and omnipotent.

However, just because our prayers do not change God, we can still believe that prayer has the power to transform. Craig Barnes puts it this way: "It isn't that our prayers are powerful enough to bring about changes. They are no more powerful than we are. It is God who is powerful. We may not know God's will, but we can be certain that God's power will change us, will transform us."[3] Because we are mortal and our perspective is necessarily in time, it may seem to us that God "answers" or responds to prayer, but actually, we are often the ones who have changed. We should pray because Jesus told us to do so; but even more importantly, we pray because Jesus prayed himself, and we are called to *become* like Christ. Calvin called this sanctification: the process of patterning our lives on Christ's example. In the garden of Gethsemane, Jesus prayed for God's will to be done, not his own (Matt 26:39; Mark 14:36; Luke 22:42). Prayer, therefore, can change our perspective and interpretation of events; prayer can even transform our experience of the world.

This idea of transformative prayer is not limited to theology. In today's medical community, there is a significant amount of research involving "mindfulness." By this term, healthcare professionals and scientists generally have in mind practices like prayer and meditation. Norman Doidge, a doctor who has researched new theories regarding the brain's ability to change, has documented that meditation teachers have thicker parts in certain areas of their brain due to their spiritual practices.[4] There is a growing amount of evidence that periods of prayer, even as little as thirty minutes every other day, can actually change the composition of one's brain.

2. Calvin, *The Institutes*, 891.
3. Barnes, *Sacred Thirst*, 54.
4. Doidge, *The Brain that Changes Itself*, 290.

While the scientist proves that prayer literally changes you, perhaps the theologian claims this change is the Holy Spirit working within you. In praying for rain, I am not changing the mind of God. Neither is God withholding rain until a certain percentage of people pray hard enough or until the "right person" prays. But prayers for rain have the advantage of making me aware of my environment. As I prayed for rain during our summer drought in Dublin, I noticed the brown grass. This reminded me of the plight of farmers whose livelihood depends on water to sustain their crops. I became aware of the need for rain and was mindful of the needs of others in my community. And so I prayed for our farmers and sought them out to offer encouragement and words of hope. Through our prayers, I do not believe that we hastened the coming precipitation; because of our prayers, I think that we were more thankful when rain finally fell.

SOMETHING SPECIAL

BJ is a member of New Dublin who has been living with multiple sclerosis for twenty years. She often says that MS is "not my best friend." Her understated humor belies an inner strength that has remained, even as the steady onslaught of the disease has robbed her of activities that she used to enjoy. First, she had to quit her job. Then, she couldn't hike or work in the garden. As for her diminished role at New Dublin, she went from being too tired to sing in the choir to being too worn out to even attend worship. Today, BJ is confined to a wheelchair. We try our best to bring our church to her.

During one pastoral visit, she wanted to talk about fear. She was afraid to perform even limited activities, such as sitting outside on a sunny day. She literally was afraid to move. But to her credit, she was not afraid to look within in order to find out why.

BJ asked me for spiritual advice, and I responded that she could pray for God's protection. I meant that, if she was afraid, she could ask God to watch over her and keep her safe. I read her one of my favorite psalms, "The Lord is your keeper; the Lord is your shade at your right hand" (Ps 121:5). This is a beautiful psalm, but I should have known that BJ is too smart to be satisfied by a single Bible verse.

She responded with a question about the exact function of prayer: if she didn't pray for protection, did that mean that God would harm her instead? Unless she specifically asked for it, would God keep her safe? If she did pray, would God suddenly decide to step in and keep her from injury?

The first task of a theologian is raising the right questions. In trying to help BJ think theologically, I found myself saying that, if she prayed for courage, then she might find the courage that was already inside her—courage that was a gift from God. I threw in that last part for good measure. Truthfully, I was somewhat at a loss to know how to respond to my friend. After all, I did not have a terminal illness. What did I know?

BJ replied that my advice sounded like the saying, "God only gives us the things that we can handle." I nodded hesitantly, thinking of a similar saying in Paul's letters (1 Cor 10:13).. Part of me was relieved to have given her some kind of answer, but such greeting card theology has always made me uncomfortable. The truth is that some people cannot "handle" the horrific or tragic circumstances that they experience. Most importantly, I don't believe that God places evil trials upon people (Jas 1:13–17). What could I say to her? I started praying myself.

Suddenly, I was reminded of a text that I had preached months ago about Jesus' exorcism of a demon (Luke 8:26–39). I told BJ that she had not felt like herself because of the fear and then suggested that this was similar to the biblical belief concerning demons. It sounded to me like a sinister force had gripped her. Suddenly, her eyes lit up! I told her that we could pray for God to expel the fear from her. We prayed together.

Weeks later, she informed me that she was doing much better. We shared a laugh about our "exorcism." But then BJ turned serious. She told me that she had read some of the accounts of Jesus expelling demons and that she was struck by the fact that Jesus asked for the demon's *name*. She told me that naming the fear was helpful. She said that she specifically prayed for "my fear" to leave and that she was feeling more confident.

We could analyze this account from a modern psychological or medical standpoint; perhaps naming her fear helped BJ to overcome it, or maybe the time spent in meditation actually strengthened part of her brain that helps control her anxiety. I couldn't answer those questions, but as her pastor, I am interested in the implications of this story towards an understanding of prayer. Is BJ's story an example of "magical" prayer? What does this experience tell us about the role of prayer in our lives?

Ultimately, I think this experience with BJ points to "something special." Let me explain:

Another member of New Dublin, Mary Jem, spent an entire month in the hospital because she had suffered a stroke. Yet she still considered herself blessed. The truth of the matter is that she would not be alive today had it not been for the actions of another parishioner named June. But this is also a story about prayer.

During my first summer at New Dublin, June was nearly ninety years old and almost completely blind. She was able to live by herself in a small apartment thanks to the kindness of her friends, including Mary Jem. Mary Jem says that her relationship with June started with a special feeling she had one day. She claims that "something" told her to go and see June. So she brought two milkshakes to June's apartment and read the paper out loud to her. A real and lasting bond developed from such inauspicious beginnings. Mary Jem took care of June's physical needs, like buying her groceries, answering her mail, and writing checks. More importantly, she was loyal, kind, and as sweet to June as the milkshakes she often brought with her. Little wonder, then, that June refers to Mary Jem as "my angel."

Mary Jem called June one afternoon as per usual. This time, however, June insisted that her friend spend the night with her. All of southwestern Virginia was suffering through the hottest month in recorded history, and Mary Jem did not have an air conditioner. (She insists to this day that it makes her nose run.) At any rate, Mary Jem agreed to come and spend the night in June's air conditioned apartment. It was hot enough to put up with the need for Kleenex!

Hours passed and yet Mary Jem did not arrive. Under normal circumstances, June probably would not have worried. Mary Jem is legendary in Dublin for going out of her way in order to help other people, which is a beautiful habit that sometimes makes her terrifically late. But "something" told June that this time was different. She called the superintendent of her apartment complex and convinced him to check on Mary Jem. He found her unconscious on the floor and immediately called the paramedics.

I have since been told that every hour a stroke victim goes untreated makes it all the more difficult to recover. The fact that Mary Jem was talking with me only a few weeks later is testimony to the importance of June's phone call. They both know this fact. During one of my hospital visits, I let Mary Jem use my cell phone to call and thank June for saving her life. June had become an angel for Mary Jem.

The lives of these two women are so closely intertwined that I sometimes pray for "Mary June" without even realizing my mistake. Their love for each other is a connective force that binds them together. After she came home from the hospital, I picked up June and we went to Mary Jem's house in order to surprise her. However, Mary Jem swore that she was expecting us that afternoon: "something" told her that we were coming. Perhaps it is the same "something" that told Mary Jem to visit June and then worried June enough to check on Mary Jem. Maybe the "something" prompted me to mention the exorcisms of Jesus to BJ and inspired her to study those passages on her own. Maybe that "something" works through prayer.

TOWARDS A THEOLOGY OF PRAYER

One of my favorite tactics that I picked up in graduate school is entitling a paper "towards" a topic, as I have written in the above subheading of this chapter. If you are working "towards" something, you do not have to arrive at the answer definitively. The trick is to leave a little wiggle room! Towards a theology of prayer, I want to make some conclusions, yet still leave plenty of room to acknowledge the mystery.

Norman Solomon notes that the standard Hebrew word for prayer (tefilla) derives from the lexical root which means "to judge." Solomon concedes that such "judging" correlates to a form of introspection, which can lead to the transformation of our minds and attitudes. But Solomon also points out that Rabbi Abraham Joshua Heschel dismissed the notion of prayer as merely another form of self-development. Solomon summarizes that, while "prayer undoubtedly modifies the internal reality of the one who prays," many prominent Jewish thinkers like Heschel, "still believe that God modifies external reality in response to prayer."[5] Accordingly, many people, clergy and lay, believe that prayer is more than just another self-help strategy for individual improvement.

When I attended a writing workshop at the Collegeville Institute, my colleagues pressed me towards a deeper understanding of prayer precisely on this point. They agreed that it was important to concede the ultimate mystery of prayer, but they were unwilling to let me off the hook that easily. One asked, "What about my desperate 'help me' prayers in the shower?" Another shared that, when told by others that they have

5. Solomon, Judaism, 96–97.

been praying for him, he honestly replied that he "felt" them. It seems that prayer can help a person with his or her internal struggle concerning their diagnosis of cancer, but what about a prayer for *healing*? Like Heschel, do we believe that God modifies external reality in response to prayer? What about prayer as a means to transform our situation or even the world around us?

The stories I have related in this chapter do involve the question of prayers for healing. It is certainly true that we prayed for Mary Jem to recover from her stroke; it is just as true that she did recover. To this day, she and I thank God for her healing nearly every time we see each other. In addition, I pray for BJ's healing down to this very moment. There is certainly nothing wrong with this prayer: I think it is honest. Of course, we want BJ to be healed. And what does it mean to be faithful if not to speak the truth?

Every Sunday at New Dublin, we take time to share our prayer requests out loud as a congregation. During this prayer time, you had better believe that we pray for external reality to be modified! We pray for healing from illnesses and for an end to war. We pray for children to be fed and for good weather. We want to be healed, we want our world to be safe, and we want God to do it. So we pray.

Yet, as every praying person knows, God "answers" our prayers in ways that may not be what we expect or want. It is true that Jesus taught us to pray for God's will to be done. And God's will is not necessarily our will, is it?

I do not claim to understand how prayer works because I do not know the mind of God: "How weighty to me are your thoughts, O God! How vast is the sum of them!" (Ps 139:17). But I do believe that, because God is all-knowing and all-powerful, God's *love* never changes nor leaves. I do not say this blithely: I realize that God can seem distant. Our questions can seem to open up a chasm between us and God. Yet when God seems far away, I try to remember that my prayers are always "heard" because God's love is always present. Just as God became flesh and lived among us, so Jesus promised that the Holy Spirit would be with us as a comforter no matter what we experience (John 14:15–27). The promise is God's presence.

In light of the promise of God's presence, it is important to realize that the Lord's Prayer begins with "Our Father." We do not pray to a distant deity or a cruel tyrant any more than we actually believe that God is male. The meaning of "Our Father" is that, since God is our loving creator and gracious provider, we are brothers and sisters to one another. We do not face our questions alone. Taking nothing away from the significance of individual prayers, it is important that we pray as the body of Christ. We need prayer time during corporate worship. We need to share our hopes and our joys, our requests and our concerns. In truth, I have found that the act of praying together can be more meaningful than the words themselves. This is a mystery, but it seems to me that it is also a hope.

Quite frankly, prayer remains a hopeful mystery to me. I do resist certain theologies of prayer because of my beliefs about the unchanging nature of God. On the other hand, I claim by simple faith that God's love is never lost or ever absent, even if experience points to the contrary. Especially through difficult circumstances, I believe with my whole heart we should pray for one another and, just as importantly, that we should pray together. For the only way we can experience the eternal one is in the present. God is that special "something" that we feel with one another, guiding us one moment and comforting us the next. I know that we should pray because, no matter where we are or what we must endure, we can suddenly be reminded that we are with people we love. Gratefully, we add our voices to the chorus of saints that sings of the mystery of God throughout the ages and forevermore. All that is left to say is simply "amen."

"HOMECOMING PRAYERS"

July 25th, 2010
Luke 11:1–13

"O Lord, teach us to pray!"

These are the words on the lips of Jesus' own disciples, and I am grateful that they have been handed down to us. The desire to learn how to pray is just as much on the minds of twenty-first century disciples as it was all those years ago. O Lord, teach us to pray, *too*!

If prayer is something to be taught, and thereby something to be learned, it is surprising that these original disciples would ask this question. They were Galilean Jews who were devout and religious. They were familiar with the great prayers recorded in Scripture, had memorized what to recite before meals, and knew the beautiful blessings to pray at funerals. These prayers were common knowledge among men and women in Jewish culture, just as the Lord's Prayer is common knowledge here at New Dublin. So if the disciples already knew many different prayers, what were they really asking of Jesus? Indeed, what are we really asking today?

I think that the disciples were asking about the deep mystery of prayer. How can we mortals communicate with the immortal God? Just what do we think we are doing when we seek the one who created us?

Because they desired to probe the mystery by pulling back the veil between us and God, the disciples looked to Jesus as a special teacher of prayer. After all, Jesus had a special relationship with God. I think that "teach us to pray" really means "teach us, Jesus, how to love and trust God the way that you do." Jesus referred to God in the most familiar of terms, as "Abba" or "daddy." I think that the disciples yearned for that same kind of relationship to the all-powerful and all-knowing God. I know that I do.

In response to their request to learn how to pray, Jesus teaches the disciples a prayer of love and trust known as the Lord's Prayer. Our text this morning is from Luke, but it shares much in common with Matthew's well-known version. Jesus teaches that God is the Holy Ruler whose kingdom shall come and be established on earth. He also instructs us to pray for the basic things that we need, such as bread, forgiveness, and guidance. In these ways, the Lord's Prayer is a deeply personal prayer that lacks formalities. It is a prayer to "Our Father" who is an intimate friend and a powerful provider. Jesus teaches that prayer is a conversation with the creator of the universe who hears our cries for help. To pray such a prayer is to freely admit our need and to profoundly trust that God will answer us.

Ah, but here is the question that keeps me up at night: What, then, does such a prayer *do*?

There was once a tornado that ripped through a little church in the Midwest. At the time of the disaster, the children's choir was rehearsing. From his office window, the pastor saw the tornado approaching and he quickly gathered all the kids into the main hallway. They huddled together as the winds tore the church apart all around them. While I don't think that they prayed the Lord's Prayer, they did hold hands and sing,

"Jesus Loves the Little Children." The tornado destroyed the building, but no one from this little prayer circle was killed.[6]

That is a powerful image of prayer! Should we end the sermon right here?

As we are all well aware, such stories do not always end so happily. Children are injured in car accidents, tornadoes, and all manner of tragic disasters. People pray their hearts out, and yet, loved ones still die. It is one thing to talk about a loving God when we receive what we have asked for in prayer. What about *unanswered* prayers? What about prayers that are answered in ways that we did not expect or want?

It seems to me that two things must be said. First, whether we are praying for rain in the midst of a dry spell or for protection in the middle of a tornado, God already knows our situation. God is not like an emergency response team that needs to receive a phone call in order to act! Secondly, while God knows all, we are not God. There is much that we cannot understand. Accidents and disasters are mysteries. There are questions of innocent suffering that are ultimately beyond our comprehension.

But even as we acknowledge the mystery, we cling to our hope. Even in the face of unexplained tragedy, we can support one another. Notice that the Lord's Prayer is made up of petitions that are plural. Give *us* daily bread; forgive *our* sins; lead *us* not into temptation. God does not need to be told what to do nor does God need to explain everything to us; but we still need to pray *together*. Huddled against the storms of life, we cling to our faith and hold onto to one another. We pray to "Our Father" who really does love all the children of the world.

As we think about prayer, it is thereby important to talk, not only about who God is, but about who we are. On this homecoming Sunday, it is even more appropriate to think of our Presbyterian belief that there are ties that bind. Whether you come to New Dublin every Sunday or have traveled back specifically for this service, we are all bound together by our God—our God who is eternal and has no past or future. To pray is to be present—to experience God's *presence*—and by becoming present, we find a connection with those around us and those who came before us.[7]

6. Barnes, *Sacred Thirst*, 147.
7. Keating, *Intimacy with God*, 156.

I am sure that you have your own recollections of prayer with certain people. For those who have traveled back to Dublin to join us today, I imagine that this church is filled with these memories. For me, familiar prayers call to mind people I've prayed with and the situations we experienced: my father, mother, and brother with our heads bowed at the dinner table; the youth group, joining hands in a circle; the people of New Dublin at my ordination, their hands pressed on my head as I knelt in the front of this sanctuary.

Most recently, our community at New Dublin has been praying for Mary Jem. We are praying for her wholeness and healing from her stroke. I do not pretend to know why our kind and generous friend suffered from such a tragic accident. But I do know that Mary Jem wouldn't be alive today if her friend, June, had not called for someone to go and check on her. Because of June, the paramedics were able to reach Mary Jem before she died or suffered permanent injury. As I pray, without even realizing it, I find myself asking God to comfort "Mary *June*." My prayer of petition for Mary Jem's healing is tied up with my prayer of gratitude for June's rescue. Yes, there is hope! God connects Mary Jem, June, and the rest of us in prayer.

As a community of believers, we join the first disciples and ask, "O Lord, teach us to pray." That very desire and yearning binds us with faithful seekers around the world and throughout history. We cannot know all of the mysteries of our world, but we want to know God. We pray to admit that we need God; we pray to trust that God will provide for our needs. And by praying to "Our Father," we realize that we are growing closer to one another.

My friends, I have nothing left to say! Let us *pray* the Lord's Prayer . . . *together*.

5

Please Join Our Team

TEAMMATES

THE WEEK AFTER HOMECOMING marked the start of another important annual event: church league softball. I missed the first game because of a prior family commitment, but showed up early and excited for the second game. Admittedly, I was a little nervous. It is common knowledge at New Dublin that I was a baseball player, and I wanted to live up to my reputation. I am also extremely competitive. As a boy, my parents would stack the deck in my favor before card games in order to ensure my victory and prevent a temper tantrum. Of course, I've matured over the years, but deep down, I am still that child who needs to win.

One of the youth on the opposing team had arrived early as well, so I asked him, innocently enough, to throw the ball with me. I was certainly game for a little ecumenical exchange. But he was reluctant, even though we were the only two players for the next game currently at the field. When I gently pointed this out, he confessed, "Well, I throw really hard." Then he shrugged and finally admitted, "It's just that, well, sir, I don't want to hurt you."

Don't want to hurt *me*? I played college ball!

I kept such sentiment to myself, of course, but I did proceed to try and throw the ball *through* this young man's glove. Days later, my arm had still not forgiven me, and I was living testimony that pride goeth before the fall.

Thankfully, the rest of our team behaved more maturely than their pastor's pre-game antics. We had fun because we supported one another. Families from the church came to cheer, laughing good-naturedly at the

38

slow-footed runners and applauding each base hit. New Dublin *walloped* my young friend's team by fourteen runs, but my favorite part of the night occurred when our six-month pregnant player came up to bat. Sizing up Toni's condition, the outfielders moved towards the infield. She promptly crushed a towering fly ball over the left fielder's head and chugged all the way around the bases! All of us gave her a standing ovation when she crossed home plate.

Toni's heroic feats on the baseball diamond reminded me of another competitive aspect in my life. This slugging, soon-to-be mother and her husband Doug are members at New Dublin. I hoped that their leadership would encourage a number of "thirtysomethings" on our team to make a commitment to our church as well. I was aware that New Dublin members in the stands were rooting for this statistic. The addition of young couples to the church under my leadership would be even more impressive in the eyes of my congregation than my two-out, RBI single in the third inning.

Over the course of the softball season, I had the opportunity to talk about New Dublin with many young families on the softball team. All were very appreciative of this fellowship opportunity through our church. I would invite them to worship and a few accepted the offer. When they had spent about as much time in our sanctuary as they had on the softball field, I would suggest that we start praying about their family joining our membership. In response, I often heard, "Why would we want to become members at a church?"

This question, mind you, was genuine. There are many people in our society who regularly attend the same church yet never become members. I'm told that many churches no longer count membership, but exclusively keep track of attendance on Sunday morning. I will admit that, in a small country church like ours, there may appear to be little difference between a member and a regular worshipper. Our congregation is welcoming to all who show an interest, whether he or she is "official" or not. While only members can vote in congregational meetings and serve on session, a young family could certainly participate in the fellowship activities and service events of the church. I love this about New Dublin.

So then, what are the benefits of church membership? Christianity is fundamentally a team sport. I believe that joining a church is about a family making a public commitment to a community and about that community making the same commitment to that family. God has called us to be part of the mission and ministry of revealing God's love within our congregation and to the rest of the world. By God's grace, we are children of God and joining a church is part of our grateful response. Membership is therefore the public affirmation of God's work in our lives and of our commitment to discipleship with one another. Joining a church is a *celebration*: it is hitting a homerun and having the crowd cheer for you!

When I would have this conversation with my softball teammates, I always asked them to continue to be a part of New Dublin, no matter what decision they reached about membership. God binds us together in communities, not human institutions, just as we are saved by God, not by religious rituals. John Calvin stressed the significance of the invisible church, which manifests the real power of the risen Lord in the lives of believers, not between the walls of a building.

But I still want people to join our church.

It is tempting to think of new members as a celebration of the pastor's success, rather than a grateful response to God's calling. I distinctly recall a moment during my first interview with the pastoral nominating committee when an elder candidly informed me that a major responsibility of their new pastor would be to put "meat in the seats." How is the church like a baseball stadium? The point is to fill it up so that we can keep the lights on and pay the salaries!

All jokes aside, I do believe in the notion of public commitment as a response to God's grace. I am sincere about the "benefits" of membership as a celebration of the covenant of faith between new members and their church. When baptized people express the desire to join, we mark the occasion in worship with a liturgy for the renewal of baptismal vows. Everyone in the congregation is invited to reclaim their faith in Jesus Christ as Lord and Savior. While "meat in the seats" may be as good for the pastor's ego as the financial records of the church, it is much more significant that we witness to the Living God who continues to call men and women into communities. This significance is *not* measured in numbers. Rather it is shown by the love we share with one another and the larger world.

I have witnessed such love at New Dublin in deep and powerful ways. For all of his talk about putting more meat in the seats, the same elder purchased and installed an air conditioner for a sick member of our church. Such an act of service is certainly a "benefit" of being a part of our congregation. I know that she was grateful for the donation and that he was grateful for the opportunity to serve. I was proud to be the pastor of a church that reached out and cared for its members. Simply put, everybody wins; it feels good to be a part of a team.

A TIP OF THE CAP

As the summer progressed, I felt more and more confident as a preacher. In baseball terms, I was finding my swing and getting in a groove. On one particular Sunday, I stepped up to the pulpit fully prepared to knock a sermon out of the park. Just as I made my point with rhetorical flourish, however, I saw one of our newest members hurrying out of the church with tears streaming down her face. My first thought had to do with why she had left in such an obvious state of distress. That was followed almost immediately by my anxious cry: *what in the world have I done?* I worried about this throughout the rest of the service.

Immediately after church, I called her at home. I was prepared for a heart-to-heart conversation, fully expecting to explain my sermon in hopes of defusing the situation, but her husband just laughed. He sheepishly explained that she had hugged another member during the passing of the peace and had an allergic reaction to her perfume. His wife had to leave because her eyes would not stop watering! This experience should have taught me an important lesson. As is the case with any team sport, the success or failure does not rest upon only one player. The church is not just about the pastor.

A few weeks later, I was leading the congregation in reciting the Lord's Prayer when I happened to glance at the communion table. I noticed that the offering plates were missing. As the prayer continued, I reasoned that the plates were in the vestibule and that the ushers would bring them to the front. With the conclusion of the prayer, I called the ushers forward. They promptly walked to the front of the church empty-handed!

Some of the more astute members of the congregation understood that it had just dawned on me that the plates were missing. Perhaps they were tipped off by my near frantic search behind the pulpit. Soon everyone was in on the mistake. My face flushed hot with embarrassment. *What in the world have I done?*

But then a gentle chuckle began in the balcony and softly floated around the entire sanctuary. Our pianist gamely began her offertory, while her son and I jogged back into the church office to look for the plates. Our search was to no avail. The plates were not in the office either. In a sudden flash of inspiration, I grabbed my baseball cap, which was lying in my office in preparation for that week's softball games. I came back into the sanctuary and held my hat up towards the balcony, as if I was asking for tips! The chuckles swelled to full, good-hearted laugher. Two wicker baskets were substituted for the missing plates, and our pianist kept playing. Our tithes and offerings were eventually collected.

After this service, I spied a young couple, standing alone and awkwardly sipping their lemonade outside our sanctuary. This was their first time at our church. After learning their names, I took a deep breath and launched into an apology for a certain part of the service. I wanted them to know that our worship was generally more formal here at New Dublin. I wanted them to know that I *wanted* our service to run more smoothly. Yet this young man laughed off my excuses and, with a big smile, told me that he loved baseball. He wanted to know if our church had a softball team. Could he play with us?

Now it was my turn to laugh.

THE CHURCH AT ITS BEST

Richard Lischer's first call was to serve as pastor of a rural congregation. His memoir, *Open Secrets*, was a tremendous help as I prepared to begin at New Dublin, and his book is a model for this writing project. My favorite part of *Open Secrets* is Lischer's description of the "best window" of his first church.

"By the light of that window," Lischer writes, "[We] baptized babies, celebrated marriages, wept over the dead, and received Holy Communion."[1] The life of the community was celebrated underneath their best window. It served as a reminder to the community of their faith through all of the ups and downs of life. As Lischer puts it, "Our best window said, 'God is for us' and lavishly so."[2] I love Lischer's image and have sought to apply it to New Dublin.

1. Lischer, *Open Secrets*, 81.
2. Ibid., 82.

It seems to me that the "best window" at New Dublin Presbyterian Church is actually a best *picture*. Behind the pulpit, for everyone to see, proudly hangs a painting of Jesus in the garden of Gethsemane. From the beginning it was clear to me that this picture has profound significance for the people of this church. When I first visited, I learned that it was painted by a former pastor, Clyde Walsh, and given to the congregation long ago. While much has changed at New Dublin and in the world outside the sanctuary, Rev. Walsh's portrait still hangs in the same place. Just as Lischer's congregation worshipped by the light from their best window, the people of New Dublin baptize babies, celebrate marriage, mourn the dead, and celebrate Holy Communion underneath their best picture. Likewise this picture serves as a sign to our community that, no matter what, God is for us and lavishly so. We need such reminders.

In the Reformed tradition, we speak of the physical elements of communion and baptism as outward signs of invisible grace. Bread, wine, and water are symbols of God's love. Like a window or a picture in the church, these are the important symbols that direct our community towards God. As one community, we are taught by Scripture, washed at the fount, and nourished at the table. Regular participation in worship reminds us of the everlasting love of our gracious God. We are strengthened week in and week out by these constants in order to meet the challenges of a changing, even volatile world. This is the church at its best; this is the church that I want others to join.

But I will readily admit that living into such grace is a challenge.

The church is constantly waging a struggle between following Christ and following culture, between putting "meat in the seats" and professing the Son of the Living God in the larger world. Part of the struggle in mainline denominations is that not everyone finds comfort in the ancient rites of our tradition. Fewer and fewer people seem to appreciate the beauty of a best window or the legacy of a best picture. As a result, many are looking elsewhere.

My academic advisor at the University of Virginia, Valerie Cooper, has studied the rise and fall of attendance at certain types of churches. She uses the term, "seeker friendly," to refer to modern churches that explicitly reach out to visitors, particularly those with little or no previous experience in organized religion. Some of these churches are the largest and fastest growing in our country. I do not believe it is a coincidence that many of these churches look like malls. It appears that part of what it means to be "seeker friendly" is to package Christianity in marketable terms for modern Americans. According to this theology, a relationship with Jesus is the best personal investment, guaranteeing individual happiness and eternal luxury. Even if people fill the seats to hear such messages, the church should not become another manufacturer trying to market its wares in our consumer culture. It seems to me that it diminishes the gospel by reducing God's good news to a reflection of the American ideal of the individual pursuit of happiness.

Dietrich Bonhoeffer referred to "cheap grace" as "the preaching of forgiveness without requiring repentance, baptism with church discipline, communion without confession, absolution without personal confession."[3] Cheap grace conforms to society by turning Christianity into just another weekend activity. Cheap grace is about having your needs met rather than taking up your cross. Bonhoeffer understood the church at its best as a community that spoke truth to the world at all costs, and he died for his faith in a Nazi concentration camp.

While New Dublin Presbyterian Church does not resemble a mall, we have a long way to go if we are to practice our faith in terms of Bonhoeffer's personal example of *costly* grace. Therefore, rather than be purely dismissive, we might learn from the seeker friendly example in some ways. The most charitable assessment I can make regarding these churches is that they have faith in the future as a vision for expansion. It is admirable that they are reaching out to new people, and furthermore, many of their worshippers must dig deeper than the superficial appeals to personal wealth. I recognize that it is not fair for me to discount the ability of larger churches to make disciples, as if size itself was the only issue at stake. I am wary of mixing Christianity with consumer culture, but I do not wish to be understood as overly critical. We are on the same team.

As for my church, we maintain an awareness of our tradition as a means of finding strength and inspiration for today. Perhaps this is a charitable description that others could say about us, but I realize that our approach has its own shortcomings. One of our members once declared, "If the Apostles' Creed was good enough for the Apostles, then it's good enough for me!" While there is nothing inherently wrong with taking pride in tradition, it is rather intimidating for a visitor to witness the rest of the congregation rising as one and reciting the Apostles' Creed from

---

3. Bonhoeffer, *The Cost of Discipleship*, 36.

memory, especially if this newcomer did not grow up in church memo-rizing creeds. As we honor our past, I pray that we welcome people who come from outside our tradition. We are not simply trying to attract more people for the sake of filling up our sanctuary. God is calling us to tell new people about the good news of God's unchanging love.

The church at its best is about witnessing to this grace. As Bonhoeffer taught, this is a demanding call on the entirety of our lives. But there are certainly different ways for churches to inspire the same commitment to Jesus Christ. God is bigger than any model for church growth or any other box we build for Christianity. We do not have to prove ourselves to others; we can make mistakes and even laugh at them. God calls us into communities to comfort us with the familiar and to challenge us to grow. Our churches may do certain things differently, but the key is that we do not seek God alone. As members of the same team, the common factor is that we are called to be disciples, not heroes. May all churches strive to bring glory to God, instead of any pastor or member.

"HUMBLE PIE"

August 29th, 2010
Luke 14:7–14

I think that it is helpful to understand our text for today by thinking about the preceding material in Luke's gospel, specifically, the passage in which Jesus paints a picture of the kingdom of God: "Then people will come from east and west, from north and south, and will eat in the kingdom of God" (Luke 13:29). This picture is bright with all the colors of God's grace; diversity is celebrated from all four corners of the world! You might recognize that these words are repeated before com-munion. When we partake of the bread and cup at the Lord's Table, we are celebrating our hope for the future. These familiar words reassure us that, no matter how different, we still have a seat at the heavenly banquet table.

Such grace is the proper context to appreciate today's reading in which Jesus utters challenging words to those who had chosen the best places at the banquet table (Luke 14:7). Their real mistake was that these seat-stealers had forgotten they were *invited* to the feast. They were not in attendance because of their own merit or talent, but because of the generosity of the host. They had forgotten about God's grace.

I don't think that the people at New Dublin spend most of their time attempting to claim the best seats. In fact, I most often witness the opposite. I can't even count the number of times that I've visited one of our members in the hospital and discovered someone was already there. Of course, you don't visit the sick or pray with the hurting simply to impress your pastor. You are living your faith by serving one another. While Jesus spoke to people who were arrogant, I don't think that you need to hear a similar judgment.

But might you need to hear a message of *grace*?

A colleague recently shared with me a story about an encounter at the hospital. This chaplain was talking with a patient about her tragic situation and wondering how she could help this other woman. Finally, the chaplain leaned over, took both of the patient's hands, and whispered in her ear: "God loves you no matter what! You are a special person." When was the last time that you heard something similar?

In Scotland, they tell a folktale about a man who climbed the tallest peak on the Isle of Skye in order to speak to God: "O Lord," he said, "why have you been so good to the people of Scotland? You have given us these beautiful mountains and fertile valleys; you have given us sheep on the land and fish in the sea; you have given us so much. Lord, why have you been so good to us?"

It strikes me that this question is asked by many of us here in the mountains of southwestern Virginia. Have you ever felt a twinge of guilt because of the blessings that you have received? Have you looked at the suffering in the world and asked, "Why me? Why am I so blessed?"

If so, I'd like us to think about a familiar phrase in a different way: humble pie. Often this expression is used to embarrass or ridicule someone. But I'd like to offer another definition, one of grace and not judgment. Let's recognize that our blessings come from God. Let's sit at table and give thanks for the food in front of us and the family around us. To eat humble pie, then, is to accept God's grace with humility and gratitude.

To illustrate this point, another colleague once told the following story.[4] There was a young man who happened to attend a certain

---

4. This story was originally told by Rodger Nishioka at Church of the New Covenant in Atlanta and preached by Catherine Taylor at Blacksburg Presbyterian in Virginia.

Presbyterian church one Sunday. While the service was great, he thought that he wouldn't return because there was no one else his age. As he was leaving, he mentioned offhandedly to the pastor that he had just graduated from law school and was studying for the bar. This pastor seized upon this information and told him that there was a member of her congregation that could help him study for the exam. Would he like for her to set up a meeting? The visitor hesitantly agreed, figuring he had nothing to lose.

A few days later, he received a call from an older man. He went to this gentleman's house and settled down for several hours of study. The host had a remarkable grasp of the law and was a fine teacher, so they agreed to meet once a week to study together. What's more, because of this relationship, the young man started going to that Presbyterian church on a regular basis. Over several months, he developed meaningful relationships with people of all ages. When he passed the bar exam with flying colors, his church threw him a victory party at his tutor's house.

At one point during the celebration, he thanked that pastor for teaming him with such a wise teacher. She looked startled, "You know who he is, don't you?" The young man shook his head in puzzlement. So the pastor led him into a part of the house that the young man had never entered, even though he had been coming for months. As he walked into this room for the first time, his eyes grew large with amazement: the walls contained plaques, awards, and various pictures of the older gentleman with famous politicians and presidents.

"He is the former Chief Justice of the Supreme Court of this state," the pastor told her astonished young friend. "You mean to tell me that he never told you?"

"No," he whispered. "He never mentioned it."

This is a story about eating humble pie in the very best sense of the word. We gain immense satisfaction from helping one another, not for personal glory, but out of genuine concern. According to Jesus, such behavior has its own rewards: "For all who exalt themselves will be humbled, and those who humble themselves will be exalted" (Luke 14:11).

But it seems to me that the most astonishing thought is that *God* has given us gifts that we can never hope to repay. We call that grace. Our calling is to accept such grace and live in gratitude by serving others. We call that discipleship. And I don't think true disciples feel guilty.

Instead, whenever you sit down to a meal, make sure that you eat humble pie in the best sense of the expression. Give thanks to God, and then, go one step further and humbly use your gifts to expand God's kingdom on earth. Rather than seeking glory or fame, may you be just as delightfully surprised as the person in Jesus' parable who sat at the lowest place, yet heard the host say, "Friend, move up higher!" (Luke 14:10). For the good news is that they shall come from east and west, from north and south, and will eat in the kingdom of God. The kingdom of heaven is bright with all the colors of God's grace. May thanks be to God.

6

A Different Kind of Thunder

DIFFERENT ANGLES OF VISION

WHEN I WAS IN seminary, I imagined myself as a certain type of advocate for social justice. I would be a prophetic preacher who wouldn't hesitate to speak the truth, even if the truth was not popular—especially if the truth was countercultural. As I've worked in the parish, I have developed nuanced views of what it means to preach prophetically. Ironically, I have learned these lessons primarily through teaching.

One of my first major decisions at New Dublin was to start a young adult Bible study. We had four participants that first night, and these faithful ones stayed with me through nine consecutive weeks of reading the book of Philippians. Each member of the group was committed to the weekly meeting, so we could develop a routine. We gathered around a circular table, usually with dessert and coffee in the middle, and each person took a turn reading a verse from his or her Bible. Then we compared different translations; in fact, we often reread a single verse several times using different versions. Initially I was worried that this practice might be confusing, but it turned out to be very exciting. Our Bible study was a dynamic experience of encountering text in new ways. Since more than one meaning was plausible, we were exploring the rich meaning of biblical texts. One young man remarked that the various translations helped him to see Paul's thinking from different angles and therefore opened up a whole range of meanings, not only of words but of applications to his life.

When we finished reading Philippians, I asked the group to read the entire epistle and come prepared to summarize the main themes for our last session. That night we dug into strawberry pie and the Bible.

The more individuals spoke, the more apparent it became that they had learned a great deal from our study. We had an articulate conversation about the historical setting and its subsequent affect on Paul's thinking, as well as some sharp insights into specific passages. I think it was indicative of the experience that two of the class members went on to teach Philippians to the youth group later that fall. Scott and Laura felt inspired to teach others because of their experience.

I try to create the same enthusiasm about biblical study through preaching. When I am writing a sermon, I often tilt my head at an angle towards my computer, as if to get a different look at the screen. How could I look at this in another way? It seems to me that this could be a metaphor for the effect of good Christian education. Members of a congregation want to look at familiar texts for new insights. They want to wrestle with questions rather than being given easy answers. I consider it a privilege to foster this experience and give my members the chance to exclaim, "Wow! I've never thought of it that way before!"

My brother-in-law's girlfriend, Shannon, once remarked that she was frustrated by sermons full of "clichés and crescendos." She wasn't referring to her experience at New Dublin, yet I took her insight to heart. Instead of merely reiterating ideas that a congregation has heard before in a loud voice, good preaching should open new interpretations. While the goal is to point to the truth, prophetic preaching should empower listeners to reach their own conclusions, rather than insisting on a single claim of the speaker. In this case, the task of prophetic preaching truly becomes an act of trust: we must trust others in our community as biblical interpreters and, ultimately, trust where God is leading as we discern that path together.

After this rewarding experience with the book of Philippians, I began another Bible study on Wednesday mornings. I hoped to create a time specifically for retirees because I did not interact on a regular basis with this population outside of Sunday mornings. This group consists of people who are neither homebound nor active in evening events, so I do not often visit them in their homes or get to know them at softball games or potluck suppers. Yet they are some of our most committed members, faithful in both their attendance and stewardship. I hoped to give them a fellowship group and an opportunity to grow as disciples.

While a church Bible study is not a seminary classroom, members of this group are bright, inquisitive, and faithful. They are curious and *relish* new information. They do not read Hebrew or Greek, but they understand the profound implications of a meaningful word or a key concept. Mark Twain might as well have spoken for our class when he said that the difference between the right word and the almost right word was the difference between lightning and a lightning bug!

The class responds to the power of the biblical words with insightful questions and comments. When we studied the parable of Lazarus and the rich man (Luke 16:19–31), several people immediately began to talk about tithing—even though the parable makes no mention of this practice! As I brought this irony to our awareness, we realized that the text made us uneasy about the privileges we enjoy in our church and in our country. One gentleman said that, "I know that I am rich when compared to the rest of the world, but I'd really like to be let off the hook." This honesty led to a moving discussion about the crippling nature of guilt.

As a teacher of the Bible and facilitator of group discussion, I've come to appreciate the importance of pastoral relationships. Like Twain's understanding of the right word, the right sermon can strike a listener as truly life changing. Jeremiah illustrates this kind of prophetic preaching when he claims that houses and fields and vineyards shall *again* be bought in this land (Jer 32:15). The prophet does not deny the painful reality of the enemy forces at the gate, but neither does he leave the people hopeless. Acknowledging the truth of a situation does not limit the possibility of God's future.

THE POLITICS OF THE CROSS

Sermons can offer a vision of hope as a means of assurance. Yet the prophetic task must also challenge certain assumptions and unjust practices. We are told that it is not polite to talk religion or politics, but the prophets give us no choice. As Amos makes crystal clear, we must decry the abuses of power on behalf of the oppressed: "They sell the righteous for silver, and the needy for a pair of sandals—they who trample the head of the poor into the dust of the dearth, and push the afflicted out of the way" (Amos 2:6–7).

On September 23, 2010 the Commonwealth of Virginia executed a female prisoner named Teresa Lewis. Virginia had executed a man as recently as 2005, but had not carried out the death sentence for a woman since 1912. Granted, this condemned woman had confessed to a heinous act of violence. However, there was ample evidence that she was mentally handicapped. Furthermore Lewis did not act alone, yet the other convicted criminals did not receive capital punishment. It appears that this woman took the fall for the crime.

Christians can be among the foremost advocates of capital punishment. I believe that it is worth questioning the theology of this political stance. In a memorable sermon, my dad wondered what would be different today if Jesus had died on the electric chair or by lethal injection. Would we hang little silver and gold replicas of those devices of death around our necks? His point was that our church as a whole has failed to grasp that the cross was an instrument of torture and death used by the Roman state to carry out its verdicts of justice. The tragic irony is that we believe that God's own son was condemned and executed by a government, yet we live and worship in the only Western nation with legalized execution.

I know that "politics" is a dirty word in some churches and, to a certain extent, at New Dublin. As pastor of a church with the full spectrum of political opinions, I am certainly aware of the danger of using the pulpit as a bully pulpit for decisive political issues. My job is not to tell people how to vote. Separation of church and state is good for both institutions. We should, however, contextualize our experience in the world from the perspective of faith. Karl Barth once uttered a great line about preaching with the Bible in one hand and the newspaper in the other. The execution of Teresa Lewis made headlines all across the country. To ignore the headlines on Sunday morning is to render religion irrelevant, if not impotent. Preachers must strive for a third way beyond political partisanship and silence on the issues. The pulpit is neither a political campaigning platform nor an excuse to hide one's head in the sand.

It is a daunting task to navigate the tightrope between these two extremes. It seems to me that the key is to preach theology. Shirley Guthrie defines theology as the quest for the ultimate truth about God, about ourselves, and about the world we live in. After offering such an all-inclusive definition, he asks rhetorically, "What else is there to talk about?"[1] We should not preach politics, but by helping our congregations to think theologically about every aspect of their lives, faith can become relevant and inspiring. In order to do this, we need to develop our theology of the cross.

1. Guthrie, *Christian Doctrine*, 1.

The cross is not simply a golden charm for a necklace anymore than the significance of Jesus' death is only about eternal salvation. As followers of the crucified Messiah, we should interpret *all* of our experiences through the example of the one who died for us. I once heard Helen Prejean speak about the cross of Christ as one arm extended towards the victims and the other towards the criminals. Since most of us are neither sufferers nor perpetrators, we fall into the middle. We practice our faith between the innocent and the guilty. It is precisely here that we must look to the cross for guidance. Does capital punishment reflect the way of our Lord? Should we live in a country that practices the death penalty and profess our faith in a man who was unjustly executed by the state? How are we called to love our enemies?

Of course, victims need loving care and criminal actions have consequences. Nevertheless I am against the death penalty, not only in the case of Teresa Lewis, but in principle—the interpretive principle of the cross.

BREAKING NEW GROUND

One of my parishioners knows a number of jokes at the expense of pastors, so naturally he loves to tell these jokes to his pastor. In order to understand his favorite, you need to know that "new ground" refers to land that has never been plowed. It has been recently cleared of trees and therefore contains many roots still hidden in the soil.

An adolescent boy was plowing such a plot of new ground one day with a team of mules. Predictably, his plough would get stuck on the roots, and, perhaps understandably, he would respond out of his frustration with a loud curse! It went on this way all morning, the plough sticking and the boy cursing, until finally a certain pastor came walking by. He told the boy that there was no need for such language. In fact, this pastor offered to provide a model of Christian piety by leading the team of mules down and back. As this pastor worked his way with the plough, it stuck in roots in much the same way as before. Instead of cursing, however, the pastor said, "Well, I ain't never seen nothing like it!"

The pastor continued on in this way, repeating this expression many times because the plough became stuck many times. Finally, he returned with the mules. This pastor was covered in sweat but nonetheless triumphant: "See here, boy! I proved that I could plough new ground without cursing!"

"Well," the boy responded. "You might as well have been cursin' instead of tellin' all those lies!"

This joke says something important about a popular opinion concerning theologically trained pastors. People resent pastors who, out their arrogance, belittle others. In Wendell Berry's fictional Port William, the town's barber, Jayber Crow, attends a Sunday morning service and laments that he only hears, "Young students from the seminary who wore, you might say, the mantle of power but not the mantle of knowledge."[2] Jayber believes that these pastors, "Went to school, apparently, to learn to say over and over again, regardless of where they were, what had already been said too often."[3] Now that will take a young preacher down a notch or two! As the boy in the joke makes clear, the irony is that, even with all that education, we sometimes do not understand what we are talking about.

As Jayber would counsel me, I need to become a part of people's lives in order to know what to say to them. Philo of Alexandria is said to have urged his listeners, "Be kind, for everyone you meet is fighting a great battle." Rather than pointing fingers with grand self-righteousness, preachers must be willing to stand among the people. As Helen Prejean believes, we all need to stand with them in the middle of the cross, the messy intersection where there are no easy answers.

One of my seminary professors, Frances Taylor Gench, began each semester by quoting Robert Frost: "Education is the ability to listen to almost anything without losing your temper or your self-confidence." It is wonderful to be around people who are secure in their own beliefs and do not to feel threatened by other opinions. In Bible study at New Dublin, we try to live into this wisdom. In addition to learning methods of biblical interpretation, our group spends a great deal of time cultivating a supportive environment. We feel comfortable enough to ask questions that are truly on our hearts and risk sharing our deeply held convictions. Indeed, I am often amazed by the personal details that are shared. As the teacher, I come to Bible study with a lot to say; but I've found that sometimes the best thing I can do is to be silent and allow another person to share from the heart.

In all situations, I want to be pastoral to every person who comes to our church. Whether an individual happens to agree or disagree with

2. Berry, *Jayber Crow*, 160.
3. Ibid.

me, I always want to show compassion for that person's conviction. In both preaching and teaching, I try to address even contentious issues from a theological perspective. By speaking to the underlying issues at the heart of the matter, I hope to reframe the debate in such a way that we can move forward together. Such approaches may help us work through some of our pain and anger. Perhaps the real challenge to all of us is to dig deeper and sharpen our own opinions against opposing viewpoints, while we remain a part of the same community. In our current political and social contexts, such skills to facilitate relationships with those whom we disagree are truly valuable. Might such efforts even be prophetic? Without a vision, the sage writes, the people perish (Prov 29:18). I have come to believe that the prophetic task is to point to that vision from within the community as a co-participant and a co-learner in the group's unfolding experience of God.

I've already mentioned Twain's great comparison between words and lightning. The great preacher, Gardner Calvin Taylor, once spoke of preaching as reaching up and pulling down some thunder. James Weldon Johnson famously characterized black folk preachers as "God's Trombones" because of the power and beauty of their words. I do believe that such a booming homiletic style is appropriate in the mouth of the right person. Perhaps someone else could have delivered a thunderous critique of the death penalty that would have struck the hearts of the listeners in transformative ways.

But I am a different kind of prophetic preacher. I am committed to diligent study and contemplative prayer in order to discern the direction of the Holy Spirit in our modern world. I will try to offer that informed and faithful theology by standing with my people, rather than pointing my finger at them. Instead of trumpeting my opinion as the answer, I most often raise questions directed towards all of us. I am going to try and preach about the righteousness that God calls us to honor, whether black or white, conservative or liberal, victim or criminal. The cross of Christ is the intersection of difference held together by love. Without such a vision, the people perish.

"WHAT'S IN A NAME?"

September 26th, 2010
Jeremiah 32:1–15; Luke 16:19–31

Why did Jesus speak in parables? This question has bothered the faithful ever since the very beginning when it was asked by the original disciples (Mark 4:10). In response to their question, Jesus replied rather cryptically that parables had to do with sharing the mysteries of God. As we commonly say around here, "The Lord works in mysterious ways."

But that doesn't mean that we shouldn't use our God-given minds in order to try and understand the world around us. Jesus also commanded us to love the Lord with all our heart, soul, and mind (Matt 22:37; Mark 12:30; Luke 10:27). Mysteries exist, but we need to think hard about our faith.

The point of a parable is precisely in this idea of faith seeking understanding. A parable is not meant to give an easy answer; rather a parable challenges us to contemplate mysteries, to think outside the box, to consider our faith from a different angle, and perhaps even to change our point of view.

If a parable is supposed to challenge us to think, then we do the parable of Lazarus and the rich man a grave injustice by simply reducing it to a matter of the rich versus the poor. Certainly, those with resources should share those resources, but I think that this parable has more to say than simply shaming us to put a dollar into an empty cup. I once heard a fitting image for this type of shaming preaching: it is like dropping a load of guilt from a dump truck on your head! I want us to move beyond this "dump truck" theology by interpreting the parable as a message of symbolic action.

I started thinking about symbols because of our other biblical passage this morning. Though he is in prison and his city under attack, the prophet Jeremiah buys a field. If you think that our housing market has suffered, imagine the value of land when an enemy invades! What is Jeremiah thinking? His actions make no sense. Yet Jeremiah buys this field and puts the proof of sale into a clay pot to symbolize *hope*: though Judah will fall to the invaders, "Houses and fields and vineyards shall again be bought in this land" (Jer 32:15).

Symbols can convey abstract meanings, like hope, because of two characteristics. First, a symbol is concrete and tangible. You can reach out and touch a symbol. But secondly, a symbol represents something else, something that might even be intangible like an idea. This understanding of the dual nature of a symbol is important because Jeremiah's purchase of the field is not the only symbol in the text. In the Hebrew language, certain names have specific meanings, much like we name children "Hope" or "Charity" in our culture. In Hebrew, however, a person's name can mean an entire phrase. In the same passage from Jeremiah, Hanamel translates into "God has pitied," Neriah means "The Lord is a lamp," and Mahseiah, "The Lord is a refuge." These names are not fancy word games; they are spiritually profound. Hope is symbolized in the very names of the messengers.

If a name is symbolic of a belief about God, then one has to think really hard about a particular story or parable. As part of loving our Lord with all of our minds, we can think of our parable in Luke's gospel in such a symbolic way, as representing both a concrete story and a deeper meaning behind a story. It seems to me that, since Jesus knew Hebrew and taught in parables, the name "Lazarus" is significant, especially since this man is the *only* character in any of the parables that Jesus told who was given a name. It turns out that Lazarus is the Greek form of the Hebrew name, Eleazar, which is translated "God has helped."

What is the significance of "God has helped" as a name?

If we thought hard about it, then we might believe that God is still helping people despite horrible conditions. We might conclude that we shouldn't overlook people in need because they too are recipients of God's eternal love and care. We may even reason that our journey in this world is ultimately not about materialism or works of righteousness, but about testifying to God's grace that is freely given to those who cry out for help. If we continue to ponder these meanings, we might wonder how the message of God's help applies to life today.

Studying the Bible is important, not merely to learn Hebrew word games, but so that we can interpret our experiences in the world. What if this parable is not simply about the punishment of the rich man? What if the point is not to pour out a dump truck of guilt on our heads? What if there is a deeper meaning symbolized in the parable?

The Commonwealth of Virginia recently executed a woman named Teresa Lewis. How might the image of Lazarus, the person who God helped, help us to think about this current event? Since God sides with Lazarus, who might we side with? Does the parable encourage us to act with an eye for an eye and a tooth for a tooth? Or does the message of God's grace encourage us to give grace to others? What is the significance that the man who told this parable is the same Jesus executed by the Roman state on the cross?

Now you could respectfully disagree and even claim that I'm reading too much into the parable or applying it in the wrong way. That's fine; in fact, I raise these questions to encourage you to think for yourselves. The beauty of a parable is that we can think in different ways and even reach different conclusions. Certainly there are many valuable messages in the parable about Lazarus, and, likewise, there are many ways to apply these messages to our lives today.

Therefore I am not trying to give you the answer about the question of capital punishment any more than I am insisting on one interpretation of the Bible. Jesus told parables to encourage conversation; he wanted his disciples to think about God's mysterious presence in the world around them. As a follower of Jesus, I preach to start a conversation among a modern community of disciples. I invite debate, rather than seeking to shut it down.

But I am concerned that too many are thinking too much about guilt. I worry about the decisions made by people who are buried underneath an avalanche of guilt from dump truck theology. Shackled by guilt to our own circumstances, it is difficult to place ourselves in someone else's shoes. I wonder if that was the problem of the rich man in the parable. Was he so burdened by what he had that he couldn't see another's load? Was he so weighed down that he couldn't lift a hand to help or to reach out in compassion?

My message to those buried in guilt is that God reaches out to you. Whether or not your name is Lazarus, God has helped you. Because of this grace, we are asked to help others, not out of guilt but gratitude, not from fear but love. For the same God who promised hope through the symbolic actions of Jeremiah is the same God who raised Jesus from the dead as the ultimate sign of our salvation.

So just what is in a name?

The name, Jesus, means "God saves." Therefore, we do not always have to agree because our hope is in God, not in our own thoughts or actions. But by wrestling with the questions, we seek to discover our Lord's mysterious ways, even in a violent and confusing world. Freed from guilt, may we help one another with the task of interpreting Scripture. As God has lifted our burdens, may we help one another make sense of our world. May we think about our faith in order to guide our understanding. And, though we may disagree about any number of interpretations and issues, may all of God's people say, "Amen."

7

Named by Grace

WORSHIP AND WONDER

THE IMAGE OF JESUS welcoming the little children reminds me of Fred Rogers. I've read that this late Presbyterian pastor maintained the same weight for virtually his entire adult life: 143 pounds. Not only was he health-conscious, Mr. Rogers also liked the number 143 because he said it symbolized, *I love you*—a phrase composed of words with one letter, four letters, and three letters. I like to imagine Jesus as a similar embodiment of childlike love.

More to my purpose, however, are the practical applications for children, youth, and adult ministries. I am reminded of Fred Craddock's advice to young pastors. Craddock believed that, at the bottom of every page of every sermon, we should pencil in the question, "So what?" So what are the implications of Jesus' call to welcome children for our lives? As a pastor, this raises even more questions for me: what might we learn from the experience of children in our churches? How might we encourage their spiritual growth? And, to recall another of Jesus' famous sayings, how might we adults have the faith of a child?

It seems to me that one way to begin to address these questions is to consider the activities in our churches that include both adults and children. Specifically, I am thinking of a meaningful liturgical practice known as the passing of the peace.

The passing of the peace is an ancient Christian rite. Typically a worship leader will say to the congregation, "The peace of Christ be with you." Then everyone replies, "And also with you." After this corporate response, time is usually set aside for individuals to greet those around them. While the liturgical refrain and ritual practice are generally the same, the peace can take place at different points in the service. For instance, the church that Ginny joined in Richmond exchanged peace as the very last part of the worship service. In some ways this makes perfect sense, as greeting one another naturally leads into the fellowship after church.

In most churches, however, the passing of the peace immediately follows the assurance of pardon. This is the liturgical order reflected in the Presbyterian *Book of Common Worship*. After we have confessed our sin and been assured of God's grace, the community has confidence that we are in a right relationship with God. As a result of this grace, we welcome our neighbor whom we are also commanded to love. Although this practice can appear more like a "meet and greet" than solemn worship, we need to remember that the triune God consists of an active *relationship* between the Father, Son, and Holy Spirit. Therefore, worshippers should also be in relationship with one another. Passing the peace is a key moment in any service of worship: it is *not* a brief intermission, temporary timeout, or seventh inning stretch!

I was strongly in favor this theology, and initially assumed that I would continue the practice at New Dublin of passing the peace at this point in the service, but before I came to New Dublin, I had not considered the role of children in worship. I had assumed that they would sit in church and shake hands with everyone else at the appropriate time, just as I did when I was growing up. It is sobering to realize what we take for granted as a faith community, especially when dealing with our children.

The children at New Dublin, however, have their own service called "Worship and Wonder." This is a children's church program that runs simultaneously with the Sunday morning service. Years before I arrived, Margaret and Diane made this their ministry, attending training conferences and workshops, and faithfully leading the children every Sunday morning. Thanks to their dedicated service, children from kindergarten to the fifth grade experience worship in hands-on and engaging ways. Worship and Wonder includes all the different parts of the order of service, including the confession, assurance of pardon, and a "feast" that is patterned after Holy Communion. I think it is important and meaningful for our children to learn about our sacraments before they are confirmed. I'm told that they also like eating extra portions of the communion bread!

Not only do they get a snack as part of Worship and Wonder, our children get to act out the biblical stories with handmade crafts donated by different members of the church. This chance to play relates to the "wonder" aspect of the program's title. Such craftsmanship also highlights the remarkable ways different people have contributed to our children's program. Indeed, Diane often marvels that every time an item is needed for the ministry it happens to appear in the classroom. It is important that adults have the opportunity to contribute in different ways to the same program. Clearly, we value our children in their worship and in their wonder, appealing to different learning styles and engaging our children with age-appropriate lessons.

There is only one problem with this model. Children's church has a tendency to become separate and distinct, thereby promoting divisions among the body of Christ. To their credit, Margaret and Diane have consciously incorporated Worship and Wonder into the rest of the church, such as using the same responsive liturgy in their classroom that we use in the sanctuary. I think it's great, for example, to greet one of our children by saying, "the Lord be with you" and hear the response, "And also with you."

But for the program to run effectively, the children need to have about as much time in their classroom as the service in the sanctuary. This meant that the children would gather on the first pew for the announcements and read the call to worship with the rest of the congregation. But then, as the opening hymn began, the children filed quietly out of the door. Mind you, I appreciated their well-behaved exit as much as I thought it was important to have a program designed just for their age; but there was no formal acknowledgement of either their presence or their departure. It was as if the children were never really a part of the service with the adults. It was Ginny who first pointed this out to me, but this lack of inclusion was not lost on the children either.

One Sunday before worship, a precocious and extraverted child named Grace had taken it upon herself to serve as New Dublin's unofficial photographer. She skipped around the sanctuary with her mother's digital camera slung around her neck. In between snapshots, she stuck her hand out for a firm handshake and introduced herself to visitors. I happened to overhear her say, "Hi! My name's Grace! But you wouldn't know that because children don't get name tags at this church."

She said this statement in a matter-of-fact tone of voice, yet I winced. My cursory glance around the sanctuary confirmed her statement. While all of the adults had affixed their name tags to the front of their shirts and tops, not a single child wore a counterpart. Quite frankly, I had not noticed this myself, and I am sure that there were some financial reasons for this omission. But what does it mean that this child of the church has recognized that she is in some way *nameless*? Is she not as much a part of the church as the adults? Is she not as much a part of our covenant to God and to one another? Have we failed Jesus' command to welcome her?

Thanks to Grace's insight and initiative, the eyes of adults were opened. We gave those children name tags. In addition, we thought about ways to include the children. As a consequence, the worship committee adjusted the order of the service. Because the children must leave at the beginning for Worship and Wonder, the passing of the peace now follows the call to worship. Instead of quietly filing out to their classroom, they come to the front of the church and say, "May the peace of Christ be with you." Margaret and Diane even taught them to simultaneously sign these words in American Sign Language. The rest of us respond, "And also with you." Then young and old greet one another by name. From a liturgical standpoint, the peace is a continuation of our opening praise of the glory and majesty of God: part of our worship of our Creator is that we welcome each other as creations, fellow creatures and co-participants in the kingdom of God on earth. As a bonus, everyone also gets to receive a hug from Grace and the rest of the children! More than one visitor has commented to me afterwards that they appreciated the warm welcome at the start of the service.

This story might give us warm, Mr. Rogers-like feelings, but to return to Craddock's question, *so what?* So what does all of this mean? Is the order of our worship service something trivial for pastors to bore their worship committees with? Are we just looking for excuses to parade our cute children in front of church?

As the year progressed, Grace continued to take pictures with her mother's digital camera. She has a knack for making adults smile, including her often distracted pastor. She has a beautiful way of calling my mind back to the present moment. But even more importantly, Grace practices her faith: she began a ministry of welcoming other children.

There was an only child who started attending our church with her mother. Though Cate was much younger, Grace took it upon herself to befriend her. She took her by the hand, led her up to the front of the church, and showed her how to sign the words to the passing of the peace with the rest of the Worship and Wonder group. Week after week, Grace voluntarily reached out in this way until the Sunday when I baptized Cate. On that day, Margaret and Diane led the children back into the sanctuary from their classroom. Grace stood beside her friend as I welcomed her to the family of faith with water on her forehead in the name of the Father, the Son, and the Holy Spirit. This was worship and wonder for the entire congregation.

In my own experience of worship, I often *wonder* (in both senses of the word) if a child's leadership represents nothing less than a foretaste of the kingdom of heaven. It seems to me that one of the amazing and mysterious aspects of this kingdom is that it is already here among us. We believe that God's reign broke into human history, just as Jesus walked the earth. Like the disciples who passed the peace with the risen savior, so we believe that we can experience God in our world. This is part of the reason why we come to church in the first place. Our young teacher, Grace, understands this theology more deeply than words. She understands that the wonder of worship is about taking pictures and holding hands. The point is to be present and open to the moment. She has taught me that an experience of God can take many forms, from a greeting in the name of Christ to the playing of children.

While on vacation, Ginny and I had occasion to visit a walking labyrinth at the University of Edinburgh. Designed in the style of the Chartres Cathedral in France, this outdoor labyrinth was tucked away in the beautiful grounds of the campus. It affords all visitors the opportunity to walk along its designated path, winding in and out until eventually reaching the center. A labyrinth is not a maze. As I understand it, this walk is designed to encourage introspection. It symbolizes a journey to the interior of the soul with faith that God will be found there. For this reason, I prayed at the entrance to the labyrinth to center myself for a somber ritual.

When I was about halfway through my serious walk, two young children ran up to the labyrinth and raced past me, giggling all the way. In their joy, they broke out of the bounds of the labyrinth and ran laps around it, playing tag and chasing each other, ignoring the lines designating the walking path. Neither could their laughter be contained, as it spilled out in shrieks and screams all over the courtyard. While I suppose that a truly serious pilgrim would have been annoyed, I found myself laughing as well. Observing these children at play was as relaxing as any other part of the labyrinth journey. It may well have been as sacred.

Children remind us of other ways that the kingdom of heaven can be present among us. By learning from children, we adults might discover that it is just as holy to run with delight outside of the lines.

BACKPACKS AND CIDER

Not every experience that relates to children is a spiritual high or provides a sacred insight. Practices of piety and contemplation are important, but sometimes we need to welcome children by addressing the problems that they face. There is a sign along one of our highways in Dublin that states one such problem succinctly: school may go on vacation, but lunch never does. In an area where poverty and unemployment are high, a significant percentage of children who attend our local elementary school receive a free or reduced lunch. This statistic is downright scary, especially when I think of the cyclical effects of chronic poverty. No one can learn if his or her stomach is rumbling. We want each child to have the equal opportunity to be his or her very best.

Shortly before Thanksgiving, a group of Presbyterians, Baptists, Methodists, and Pentecostals came together to address this issue of childhood hunger in our community. Our ecumenical committee was formed at the impetus of the director of Christian education at the Methodist church who wanted to start a "backpack" program. Her idea was that certain children could receive an extra backpack on Friday afternoons, which would be full of enough nonperishable food to last the entire weekend. Each week, every church in our partnership would be responsible for collecting three to four specifically assigned items. We would gather on Friday mornings to fill the backpacks, and the children would pick them up on their own in the afternoon.

I think it is relevant to point out that our backpack program reflects a larger cultural concern in rural Appalachia. While eating local food is becoming more popular in different places across the country, agriculture is a way of life in Dublin. The idea of supporting local farmers is not simply a bumper sticker; it is the heartbeat of our culture. Providing food is one of the most meaningful ways of relating to each other in a place where seemingly everyone has a garden. As Garrison Keillor has pointed out, one of the results of such abundant produce is that we must lock our cars in late summer in order to keep people from leaving bags of squash on our seats! However, some acts of generosity will not be denied. Not too long after I had moved to Dublin, one parishioner called me late one evening. He immediately apologized, not due to the hour of his phone call, but because he had not offered me anything from his garden! Almost breathlessly, he inquired, "Do you have enough *vegetables*?" I'm sure that he was aware of the produce aisle in the twenty-four hour grocery chain; his question, therefore, was a deeper one: are people caring for me by sharing what they have?

As an answer to this question for local children, the backpack program is faithfully sustained by New Dublin Presbyterian Church and the rest of our partnership churches. Adults from all the participating churches have supplied more than enough goods. Hopefully these contributions are making a real difference in the lives of children every week. In turn, we feel that we are welcoming children in the name of Jesus. Thanks to the backpack program, our worship service now begins on the way into the church, as worshipers drop off their offerings before they find their seats. I love to watch these goods pile up in the back of the vestibule. But I hope it has been clear that I believe that children should be actively involved in ministry with adults as well. This notion of caring for others is not simply a matter of adults looking after children.

Right about the time the backpack program began, we had our monthly youth meeting. Actually, all of our children and their parents came out to enjoy the event together. Everyone was welcomed, no matter how old or how young. On this particular fall afternoon, we gathered at a parishioner's house to make homemade cider. By the time Ginny and I arrived, cider production was in full swing.

The children were picking apples as a team. The older ones climbed to the top of the tree and tossed fruit down to younger kids holding buckets below. There was general delight as the buckets were filled to the brim. Apple picking, however, was only the first step. A grinder was set up on a picnic table. With the turn of a hand crank, metal teeth on an axle chopped up the fruit into little chunks and dropped them into different buckets. One child solemnly informed me that it looked like a giant had chewed up a bunch of apples all at once and spit them back out!

From the grinder, the chunks then went to the press. A clamp was placed on top of the pieces in a special bucket, and a giant screw squeezed out the juice through an opening in the side. We collected the juice and poured it out over cheesecloth, which strained out any remaining solid material. Finally, the juice was heated in order to pasteurize it and bring out the full flavors.

Perhaps some might be wondering, "So what?" Let me tell you that warm apple cider made on a gorgeous fall afternoon by laughing children of all ages is quite possibly the best tasting drink *ever*! So what? Children mixed with the adults during all of the various points of the process. Not only did they participate, but I believe that all the different ages felt welcome. Their smiles were genuine, a telltale sign of their sense of comfort and inclusion. So what? The children made our production of cider a party—our time together was fun and festive, as well as meaningful and holy. On that evening, there was peace among all the cider makers, as we gathered for worship and wonder. So what? Every person knew that they were a child of God in this little glimpse of the kingdom of heaven on earth.

"WITH FAITH LIKE A CHILD"

October 24th, 2010
Joel 2:23–32; Luke 18:9–17

Jesus called for them and said, "Let the little children come to me, and do not stop them; for it is to such as these that the kingdom of God belongs" (Luke 18:16).

I take it for granted that this is not the first time you have heard this verse. As one of Jesus' most famous sayings, it has inspired churches all across the world to paint wall murals of him welcoming the little children. In these pictures, a bearded and smiling savior is crouching down to eye level with the lovable little ones. Maybe there are even some butterflies and flowers around them, just to make the scene as appealing as possible—and why not? It is a beautiful image, one of inclusivity, tenderness, and kindness. We all know the song, so sing with me: "Jesus loves the little children; all the children of the world! Red and yellow, black and white, they are precious in His sight. Jesus loves the little children of the world!"

I love that song and I love its message. Yet perhaps the church murals and nursery songs have diluted the truly shocking nature of Jesus' view concerning children. Because I believe that we tend to think of Jesus as Mr. Rogers, we need to understand the radically different view of children that existed in the ancient world. When Jesus lived, it is estimated that only one out of every two children survived until their first birthday. Think about those odds. With the rate of infant mortality so high, rituals for welcoming a child in the larger community took place only when he or she had reached adulthood.[1] Only as an adult did a child become a real person.

Of course, children are priceless to modern families and communities of faith; but maybe this view of children is not so hard for us to comprehend. After all, children cannot vote or work. They have limited legal rights.[2] In some sense, children become "real" in our society only when they become adults. This is even true in most churches. It's fine for Jesus to welcome children to Vacation Bible School, but what about church committees? What about session? It's good to teach nursery songs, but what about offering positions of leadership and responsibility?

Jesus said that whoever does not receive the kingdom of God as a little child, shall never enter it (Luke 18:17). With this point, it seems to me that Jesus was implying that adults can and must learn from children. As strange as it seems in our culture, our community of faith remembers the prophecy from Isaiah that a little child shall lead them (Isa 11:6).

Here at New Dublin, I am proud of the fact that our children do lead. In worship, children lead us in the passing of the peace. Every week, they assemble in front of our communion table and prompt us to welcome one another in Christ's name. Do not overlook the significance of this act! We begin our worship by lifting our hearts and minds to God; then we look to our children as models of welcoming each other in the name of our Lord. Children are exemplars of our faith. For the sake of clarity, allow me to offer an illustration. Actually, let me tell you about a picture that a child drew.

One of our Bible study groups met this past week in a church member's home. On her refrigerator is a picture drawn by a small child in

1. Ringe, *Luke*, 225–226.
2. Ibid., 226.

our church. The picture is a portrait of one our Worship and Wonder teachers, but it is unlike any person that I have ever seen. This drawing is of a huge face with a gigantic smile from ear to ear. Just above each ear, there are long arms that stretch out in either direction from the side of the head! This picture person is literally all smiles and hugs. And so, this picture offers a glimpse of the world turned upside down. Perhaps the kingdom of God belongs to children because they see smiles and hugs as the important features to show to others. That is the faith of a child that we adults are called to experience and to show to the world.

I've been thinking about adults practicing their faith this week because today we celebrate four people who are joining our church. In just a few moments, they will stand up here—in the same place that the children stand to lead the passing of the peace—and make a public confession of faith. We believe that they are responding to what God is doing in their lives and we celebrate each one of them today. We welcome each of you with open arms, just as Jesus told us to welcome all children of God.

If I could speak candidly to our newest members, I want to be crystal clear that you are joining the church as *adults*. We need you to *act like adults*! We need adult leaders who are responsible, insightful, and committed. We need you to teach Sunday school classes, to lead the youth group, and to encourage people to donate food to the backpack program. One day we may need you to become ordained as elders in our church and serve on our session.

How do we reconcile this apparent contradiction between the faith of a child and the responsibility of an adult? How can we have faith like a child and serve responsibly in an adult world?

Just before Jesus welcomed the little children in this morning's Scripture lesson, he told a parable about two very different men: a Pharisee who did righteous and responsible adult things and a tax collector who was hated by the community. According to the parable, however, it is this despised man who is made right with God. It is as though the world is turned upside down! The same power is found in our text from Joel. The prophet declares that the Lord will pour out the spirit of God, not upon the wealthy or the powerful or the pious, but upon *children*—your sons and your daughters (Joel 2:28).

It is this power to turn the world upside down that sets the context to hear the message about welcoming the little children. The point is that

God is the one who is able to bring about transformation. Neither the Pharisee nor the tax collector, neither adults nor children nor anyone else can be made righteous because of anything that they do. The spirit of God is poured out as a gift from God.

We believe that the same spirit is with the four adults who are joining our church today. And in recognition of God's gift to all, each one of us, no matter how old or how young, will have the opportunity to renew our commitments to our Christian faith and to each other.

So today, before God and each other, renew the promises of our faith. Promise to smile and to hug. Promise to trust in God and to pass the peace to all people. These are promises that we make only with the help of God who transforms our community. Inspired by the same Holy Spirit, let us work together for the common good of our church and our world. May young and old practice the faith of a little child by seeing the face of Christ in one another.

8

Songs of Hope

THE BLESSING OF A LONG NIGHT

THE CHRISTMAS EVE CANDLELIGHT service is a big deal at New Dublin. We literally had people standing in the aisles. While quantity does not necessarily reflect quality, I'll admit to taking some pride in our packed sanctuary.

But I was also keenly aware of who was *not* there.

Two men had died recently: Eddie on the day after Thanksgiving and Bud on the day before Christmas Eve. I was not the only one who missed them. The holidays will never be the same for their families. How does one deal with such a loss at times that are supposed to be celebrations? How does one grieve when so many are joyful?

I do not wish to be labeled a scrooge, but suffering is real. Death is real. Illness and tragedy do not go on vacation because we celebrate a holiday. Therefore, we should not ignore the reality of grief just because we are decking the halls.

In addition to Christmas Eve, our church observed a service of worship on the winter solstice. Our December calendars were already packed with festivities, but this event was an opportunity to acknowledge our pain. On the longest night of year, we gathered in the candlelit sanctuary for individual meditation. Other than music playing softly in the background, we sat in silence. I did provide a guideline for prayer, but ultimately each worshipper was left to his or her own thoughts. While the attendance figure was nowhere near the number at Christmas Eve, it may have been more meaningful for those who did participate. I know that it was a very powerful experience for me.

Most of the time, I fill our sanctuary with words. Words are important; through sermons and prayers, I speak about the good news of the Living Word. But, during the longest night, I sat in silent prayer. I thought about those who had recently died. Their words came to me.

Towards the end of his life, Bud was hospitalized frequently due to blood clots. When I visited one fall afternoon, I found him in a reflective mood, specifically, about his second wife, Sarah. They had met when they were both in the hospital with their dying spouses. He told me how important it was to have someone relate to his experience of grief. He smiled and said, "God threw one life raft and saved two people."

Over the past few years, they had spent winters in Florida, which is where Bud died. But Bud and Sarah had lived in Dublin while transforming an ancient house into a magnificent bed and breakfast. It was during this time when they joined our church and became beloved members. Shortly after I arrived at New Dublin, Bud and Sarah invited me to their home and gave me a small fern to represent their prayers for the growth of our church. I was touched by their thoughtfulness, but I kept forgetting to water the plant. When Bud inquired about their gift a few weeks later, I sheepishly had to admit that no one has ever accused me of possessing a green thumb! He replied, "Andrew, you might as well learn now that you will never be able to do everything right." In the quiet of the longest night service, I gratefully remembered Bud's wisdom.

Then I thought of Eddie, the gentleman who had died just after Thanksgiving. Before I became his pastor, cancer took away his entire larynx. He had to communicate with a voice modulator, one of those handheld devices that is touched to the neck to produce an electronic speech. It was hard for me to understand him at first, but we shared a common language of baseball. He referred to my first Sunday as "Opening Day." In the stillness of the sanctuary, I laughed out loud at that memory.

Not long before he died, Eddie had a spot of skin cancer removed from his nose. This outpatient surgery was relatively minor, especially when compared to surgeries he had endured already. Yet his anxiety was exacerbated by a careless dermatologist who had suggested that Eddie might lose his entire nose as a result of the operation. This offhand comment haunted him for weeks. He was already self-conscious about the hole in his throat and painfully aware that others had trouble understanding his voice modulator. The loss of his nose would have been devastating, and I'm not sure he would have ever left the house again—even to attend the church he loved.

When Eddie was wheeled back from the operation on a gurney, we breathed a sigh of relief. His nose was clearly visible underneath a relatively small bandage. I smiled and told him that his nose looked as good as ever. He gave me his trademark thumbs up sign. Then his wife, Martha, asked if I would give a blessing. So I hovered my hand just above his bandaged nose and prayed: "The Lord bless you and keep you; the Lord make his face to shine upon you, and be gracious to you; the Lord lift up his countenance upon you, and give you peace" (Num 6:24–26).

Until Eddie's death, we would conclude our visits by holding hands and repeating this blessing, his mouth moving silently as I prayed the sacred refrain. I often thought that, even though he was silent, perhaps Eddie was the one who was truly being heard. Though my blessing partner is now dead, I remembered these ancient words in the sanctuary where he once sat.

John Ames, the Congregationalist minister in Marilynn Robinson's *Gilead*, reflects at the end of his long career upon the importance of blessings. As a young boy, he baptized a few kittens: "I still remember how those warm little brows felt under the palm of my hand. Everyone has petted a cat, but to touch one like that, with the pure intention of blessing it, is a very different thing. It stays in the mind . . . There is a reality in blessing . . . it doesn't enhance sacredness, but it acknowledges it."[1] By the end of the book, Rev. Ames believed that offering a blessing was his greatest act of ministry: "I'd have gone through seminary and ordination and all the years intervening for that one moment."[2]

Especially during holidays, we count our blessings. It is important to be grateful for the things we have and the people we know. But grief is with us as well. No amount of decorations, sweets, or celebrations will ever be able to change that reality. There are no words that can ever fill the space in my life that these two men have left. Yet I was grateful for the opportunity to remember them in the silence. It is true that I am not able to do everything right, but I am glad that I made time to count the blessings of memory. I'm grateful that their words, spoken and unspoken, came back to me.

1. Robinson, *Gilead*, 23.
2. Ibid., 242.

HOLIDAY CHEER

I once heard a joke about a Scottish Presbyterian pastor who wanted to ice skate to the church on Sunday mornings. He asked his session for permission, and, after much deliberation, the session agreed to grant their pastor's request with an important caveat. They would allow him to skate, if he would agree *not* to have fun!

It is not a laughing matter to forbid fun activities at church. Yet our enjoyment must be true and real, instead of covering up our true emotions with a false sense of cheer. Laughter is cathartic only if grief is acknowledged.

Immediately after the longest night service, we shared a simple meal of soup and bread. The quiet meditation in the sanctuary was a time for individual prayer; the meal in the fellowship hall was an opportunity for us to be together. While the prayer service was somber and reflective, the meal was joyful and talkative. It was another type of blessing to acknowledge God's holiness in the meals we share with the people we care about.

The supper following the longest night service was not the only time during the holiday season that I experienced the blessings of laughter and love. Nor would it be the only lesson that I would learn. Ginny and I invited the congregation to the manse for a Christmas open house. To fully appreciate this, one needs to know that New Dublin Presbyterian puts the "manse" in *mansion.* I do not exaggerate! We live in a beautifully restored, two story, nineteenth-century farmhouse with four bedrooms, four bathrooms, a dining room, a den downstairs, an office upstairs, a large foyer with a grand staircase, and a modern kitchen. This does not even include the basement, which is roughly the size of our entire first apartment in graduate school! We love living in such a spacious and elegant home, and we wanted to show our gratitude by hosting the people who made our dream house come true.

For this celebration we purchased a ten foot tree from a local farm. This manse is too large for just any small tree. In addition, New Dublin sets up a twenty five foot tree in the sanctuary every year, so we knew that expectations were *high!* While I requested delivery of our large evergreen, I did not ask for any assistance in setting up this tree in our foyer. I figured that we could complete this task on our own, and I was partially correct. After several hours of work, the tree was standing upright in our foyer, beautifully trimmed. Ginny had made *two* trips to the drugstore for more lights and was finally satisfied. I, however, was bothered by the fact that the tree was leaning slightly to the left. Ginny told me to wait until her father arrived the next day to help; I wanted to do everything myself—famous last words!

While it took us hours to set up, I managed to bring the tree crashing down after only a few seconds. Thankfully, I was not hurt (although Ginny certainly wanted to kill me!). Sadly a few ornaments broke, including a souvenir from our honeymoon to Ireland. I was able to glue most of it back together, yet I never found the "I" in the word, "Ireland." When I received the phone call that Bud had died in Florida, I hung the "reland" ornament in memory of him and in tribute to his memorable advice: I can't do everything.

With the help of Ginny's family, we fixed the tree and decorated each room in time for the open house. Even with the snowy weather, we had a great turnout after Sunday morning worship. At one point, I looked at our dining room table, filled with food and surrounded by people. I flashed back to our welcoming potluck at the church and was once again reminded that our cups runneth over. After I received several compliments on our tree, I looked over at Ginny and she smiled. All was forgiven and, yes indeed, we are blessed to share life with others.

In fact, the Taylor-Troutmans were blessed to host another large event that year. Since Christmas was on a Saturday, I could not leave Dublin due to my worship responsibilities the next day. Rather than break their tradition of spending Christmas Eve together, my wife's family decided to come to us. *Seventeen* people drove from North Carolina to spend Christmas Eve and Christmas morning with us. Admittedly, they were a big reason that the sanctuary was filled to capacity for the candlelight service. Since we did not have room in the manse for so many people, several relatives spent the night at a special bed and breakfast just down the road. I know that Bud would have *loved* that!

While I thoroughly enjoyed every person who came to visit, I could not help but notice yet another absence. My brother-in-law had dated a young woman for over two years, and we had all grown close to her. I felt her absence was especially poignant at Christmas. Of course, she is not dead. It was in their mutual interest to separate and both of them are doing well today. Nonetheless, I grieve her loss. One of my favorite memories of her was at a benefit concert that we attended together in

New York City. As I made reference to this experience in my sermon for Epiphany, more memories came back to me.

My prayer for those who have lost loved ones is that they, too, could remember special moments. Like my infamous experience with the Christmas tree, we can even recall difficult experiences as valuable life lessons. While I not suggesting that we should deny or cover up our grief, we can think back on these meaningful times as a way of acknowledging the blessing of someone's life and the gift of time together.

We should take time to remember because life flies by. With all of these activities, my first Christmas as a parish pastor quickly came and went. In a new year, New Dublin celebrated Epiphany and the gifts of the magi. When we remember this story, we proclaim the Emmanuel. Thousands of years after the birth of Christ, we acknowledge that God is with us in our pain and in our celebration. We take time to remember and spend more time together making new memories. We count our many different blessings.

"OUTSIDE MUSIC"

January 2nd, 2010
Isaiah 60:1–6; Matthew 2:1–12

Imagine if you will that the Gospel of Matthew has been put to music. What would the soundtrack be like during Epiphany?

The first musical note would be the sound of a beautiful hymn. I can hear "Joy to the World" playing in the background. We have the fulfillment of an ancient prophecy about the baby born in the city of Bethlehem. Nature sings, as the stars move in harmony with the fulfillment of God's promise. Expensive and precious gifts are brought to this special baby. These details are like soaring harmonies: repeat, repeat, the sounding joy!

But if we listen closely, we hear another sound, lurking in the background. This music would be ominous, low and repetitive like a big war drum. Danger lurks in the form of a paranoid and fanatical ruler, Herod, who devised a deadly plan to snuff out the threat to his rule. This is dark and scary music, full of malice and hate.

Matthew, then, is a complicated composer. His music is played in two keys: joy and fear. We hear the sounds of divine signs and evil plans, beautiful gifts and death threats. This is complex; yet perhaps such a soundtrack composed of opposite extremes is not so strange to us. While we praise the newborn king, we know that evil exists in our world. Lies are still told and children are still killed. We light our candles and raise them high on Christmas Eve, but we know of the darkness outside. Even if the sound of the war drum is only a distance echo, many of us have personal or family tragedy ringing in our ears. This time of year, cheerful Christmas music plays in the background; yet the sound in our heads is a sorrowful dirge. We grieve the loss of a job, a dream, or a loved one. Surely, we've all heard of someone who has recently experienced a type of loss.

I realize that this is not the message I am supposed to preach around Christmas. Turn on the television and look at all the smiling, happy people! Go to the mall and see all the bright display signs, advertising the newest, greatest gadgets that are sure to bring you peace and happiness all year long! What is with this talk of doom and gloom, sorrow and heartache? Have a holly, jolly Christmas. Santa Claus is coming to town! Everyone knows that we sing these songs during this time of year, right?

In the Gospel of Matthew, we've seen that the birth of Jesus is a complex melody of joy and fear, which is not the same as the music of our consumer culture. Why then, do we not immediately notice this difference? It seems to me that we are too close to the situation. We breathe the overt messages of our society's consumerism by hearing the same song and dance over and over again. It is hard to have the proper perspective when you are on the inside of a situation.

The Hebrew people thought they knew what to look for in the coming of the messiah. They thought that they knew the soundtrack by heart. They memorized ancient prophecies in much the same way as we learn favorite Christmas hymns. If you listened closely to Isaiah this morning, you know that gifts of gold and frankincense were expected to be brought to the messiah. This makes perfect sense: one brings these gifts to a king and a priest. But we all know that there were three gifts brought to the baby Jesus. What about the significance of this third gift that is not mentioned in Isaiah?

Myrrh was given by these men who are commonly known as the three kings or wise men. They are also called the *magi* from the word in the Greek New Testament. This ancient word, magi, refers to astrologers who studied the movement of the stars in order to predict the future.

Whatever we call them, we must remember that these men were *outsiders* to the Israelite community. They did not read the Hebrew scriptures; they "read" the stars. So these outsiders brought an extra, strange gift. Myrrh was a funeral spice that was used to cover up the stench of decomposing bodies. Such a gift is not appropriate at the joyful celebration! Or is it?

The word, epiphany, means a sudden revelation. An epiphany is like a light bulb turning on over the head of a cartoon character. With the gift of myrrh, the magi offer us that very same kind of revelatory experience. On that very first Epiphany, they gave a gift pointing to death at the very start of life. These outsiders knew that this newborn king's importance related, not only to his life, but to his death. The ones who should have been learning became the teachers. My friends, the amazing lesson is that God chose to reveal the divine secrets in a completely different way to completely unexpected people. Epiphany reminds us to sing old songs in new ways.

A few years ago, I was among thousands of people who attended a benefit concert in honor of the ninetieth birthday of Pete Seeger. For several hours, I listened to a parade of famous singer-songwriters perform songs in tribute to this folk legend. I heard cheerful songs and mournful songs. But there were no surprises. I had expected to hear these standard folk tunes, many of which had been written and performed by Seeger himself.

At the end of the night, Pete Seeger came on stage, wearing his trademark overalls and cap. But he had a surprise in store! He told us about a man named John Newton who was captain of a slave trading ship and later became a leading abolitionist in Great Britain. Along the way, he also wrote a song called "Amazing Grace." Tuning his banjo, Seeger told us that we would now sing all of the verses of that hymn together. You should always sing all of the verses, he said, both the familiar verses and the unfamiliar ones. As thousands of voices swelled in harmony that concert became a service of worship. Our worship was led, not by a clergy or priest, but by an outsider—an aged singer who was picking a banjo. I tell you *that* was an epiphany for me.

So let us sing all the verses all year long, both the familiar and the unfamiliar ones; let us sing in times of joy and in moments of grief. In so doing, may we remember that outsiders teach us to sing old songs in new ways. May we discover the epiphany of unexpected blessings.

9

O Pastor, What is Required of Thee?

HEALTHY SKEPTICISM

RICHARD'S ANCESTORS FOUNDED NEW Dublin Presbyterian Church in the mid-eighteenth century, and he has farmed his whole life in the New River Valley. Due to these deep roots, he comes honestly by his streak of Appalachian folk wisdom. He enjoys a well-turned phrase and maintains a treasury of favorite sayings, proudly using them in a variety of situations that draw a smile from his wife, Frances. For instance, he loves say, "If you ask me the time, I'll build you a clock." But my personal favorite is "There's always a little rain at the end of a dry spell."

Richard also has a curious mind and is well read. Our friendship began in front of his fireplace, discussing various theologians from John Calvin to John Shelby Spong. Often he would preface these conversations by requesting help for the "healthy" part of his skepticism. For example, he says that he is skeptical of the "God says" passages in the Bible. With a wry smile, he throws up his hands and exclaims, "How do we know that's what God really said?"

Both Richard and Frances have been faithful participants in our Wednesday Bible studies. While I wouldn't go as far as to say that we rehab skepticism, I do teach different methods of biblical interpretation. Often we study a single verse in reference to other sections of the chapter, the book, or even other books of the Bible. Reformed theologians call this practice the interpretation of Scripture by Scripture. Richard claims it helps his skepticism to read difficult passages in light of his favorite verse, "[God] has told you, O mortal, what is good; and what does the Lord require of you but to do justice, and to love kindness, and to walk humbly with your God?" (Micah 6:8).

But I think that Richard is right to be skeptical of easy answers. Interpreting Scripture with Scripture can be reductionist. While some texts, like Micah 6:8, are beautiful treasures, other passages are horrifically violent. Phyllis Trible refers to such passages as "texts of terror." It bothers Richard that the Lord commands David to allow the Gibeonites to impale seven sons of Saul on a hill to end a famine (2 Sam 21:1–9). This is a text of terror, and Richard is not willing to let David off the hook, even if he sings a beautiful song of faith a few verses later (2 Sam 22:2–4). It seems to me that he is right to resist any method of interpretation that simply wipes away the difficulties. Mysteries cannot be fully resolved even in the course of a lifetime of Bible study. Furthermore, our experience of this world is complicated and ambiguous; we don't need easy answers for our lives either. Perhaps a healthy *faith* includes a measure of skepticism.

Before I was hired at New Dublin, Richard heard me preach at a neutral pulpit. The pastoral nominating committee set up this occasion so that they could evaluate my preaching abilities. This was the Sunday after the devastating earthquake in Haiti, so I decided to address this tragedy. In fact, I declared to my wife that, "Any preacher who doesn't talk about Haiti doesn't deserve to be in the pulpit!" I said this despite the fact that I did not yet have a pulpit of my own.

Congregations have a way of showing kindness to guest preachers, so I received many compliments after the service, but I was particularly eager to hear Richard's response. In the interviews leading up to the neutral pulpit, he had already impressed me with his eagerness to think deeply about theology. As I was preparing my words, I had imagined astounding him with my profound insights about the nature of God in tragic circumstances. When I greeted him after the service, however, Richard merely smiled and shook my hand. He certainly did not seem blown away by my sermon.

After church, Ginny and I had dinner at Richard's charming farmhouse. In Dublin, Sunday is traditionally the biggest dinner, and Richard urged us to eat and eat. He wasn't really asking a question when he said, "Won't you have some more?" Frances is an amazing cook, so he didn't have to ask twice! After second helpings of both the main course and dessert, I settled back in a big armchair, sleepily watching the logs crackle in the fireplace.

Ever the conversationalist, Richard began a story about the former pastor of the church that hosted the neutral pulpit. Apparently, this young man and his wife had wanted to start a family. At this point, Ginny smiled at me, a subtle gesture that I'm sure did not go unnoticed. But Richard continued and told us that this pastor was active in the presbytery and did a number of good things in the community. My eyelids began to droop as I watched the fire burn.

Richard paused for a long moment. I look up just in time to see a shadow in his face like the embers had been extinguished. He said this pastor's wife became gravely ill after she gave birth to a son.

"And then," Richard said with emotion, "*She died.*"

Those two little words filled more space between us than all the heat from the fireplace.

"Let me tell you, Andrew, that I will never forget his face at her funeral. He was following her casket down the aisle of the church when he, suddenly, broke into a *smile*. How could he do that?"

Richard paused again, blinking back his tears.

"I tell you, that smile was a witness to the resurrection for me."

Earlier that day, I had delivered a sermon about God's grace in the midst of tragedy. But I believe that the word of God was proclaimed by a layman in a living room. At certain times, my teaching of the Bible may help Richard with a healthy sense of his skepticism; but I will always remember his story.

THE POWER OF STORY

In the classic Protestant proclamation from the high pulpit, a preacher identifies a specific message from a text and then teaches its truth to the congregation sitting passively in the pews below. The title of Fred Craddock's great work on preaching, *As One Without Authority*, is indicative of another view. To be clear, Craddock's approach does not lessen the importance of a sermon. The difference is the desire to empower listeners to discover their own message: "Biblical preaching means bearing the awesome burden of interpreting Scripture for the congregation to which one preaches. This does not mean that it is the preacher's responsibility to hand down a more or less authoritative interpretation for them, but as pastor-preacher, [he or she] will lead them into the experience of hearing the message of Scripture for their situations. This calls for real courage."[1]

Tom Long characterizes Craddock's view of the preacher as a "pioneer" because he or she is the first one of the congregation to discover the grandeur and beauty of a text.[2] Rather than crafting the sermon as straightforward proclamation of a specific lesson, the sermon is written as a delightful adventure through a text. Hence Craddock is correct: preaching as one *without* authority does call for real courage in order to explore the deep meaning of Scripture, and then to encourage others to begin their own exploration.

I first learned the value of this preaching style from taking Biblical Hebrew . . . of all things! As strange as it may sound, Professor Carson Brisson is a master at illustrating grammatical lessons with meaningful anecdotes. He used to tell our class, "We can't just learn Hebrew; we have to live it." I understood this to mean that anecdotes and other types of narratives afford the opportunities for personal connection. We learn more easily when we are touched by a concept or idea in a manner that relates to our experience. Allow me illustrate this point with an anecdote, just like my former Hebrew professor.

One Saturday in spring, we had a work day at New Dublin. All of our volunteers were committed to the task of cleaning the basement of the manse; yet they fell into two broad camps that I will call the "purgers" and the "restorers." The purgers arrived first and quickly loaded the contents of the basement into a trailer to haul the items straight to the dump. But before the trailer could be hauled away, the restorers came and *unloaded* the contents! Thus many of the previously discarded items made their way into individual's workshops, garages, and basements instead of the trash. On that morning, I stayed out of the fray of this "trash talk" because I simply wanted to clean basement. However, I recognize that there are good arguments for both sides. Sometimes it is an act of liberation to clear out materials and create a clean space. Other times it is an act of dedication to transform unwanted materials into useful or beautiful objects. At the end of the day, different people are going to "take home" different things, largely based on their assumptions and outlooks that they bring to the task.

---

1. Craddock, *As One Without Authority*, 128.
2. Long, *Witness of Preaching*, 102.

Likewise, the same message can be communicated straightforwardly or anecdotally, and different people are going to respond in different ways. I've had people shake my hand at the sanctuary door after the service and tell me that they really appreciated a particular point from my sermon. This would be great except that I did not make that particular point! I have told stories that have taken people to places far away from where I intended. But it is also true that people listen to sermons with their own theology in mind and simply hear what they want to hear. While such miscommunications can be frustrating, narrative sermons are ultimately worth these risks. According to Craddock, lay people have "the right and the responsibility to bring something of their own to the occasion."[3] People in the pews do not need to be spoon-fed a sermon. A narrative sermon "demands the movement from the present experience of the hearers to the point at which the sermon will leave them to their own decisions and conclusions."[4] A preacher should trust his or her listeners.

To paraphrase Professor Brisson, we can't just learn about our faith; we must live it. I preached on Micah 6:1–8 by using a story from an amazing book called *Little Bee* written by Chris Cleave.[5] I adapted the basic framework of the story cited in the footnote, but have changed the dialogue and certain details of the plot, including the names of the characters. In so doing, I tried to tell the story in relation to the Scripture. Micah claims that we must do justice, love kindness, and walk humbly with God. In other words, we must live our faith, not hear it from someone else. I want to be clear that stories are *not* told in worship for purely entertainment purposes. While the story found in *Little Bee* is certainly poignant, the goal of a sermon is to connect our stories as individuals and communities to God's story. We need to view our experience of the world in light of our faith. I trust that a story in the form of a sermon allows people to draw their own conclusions that are likely to be more meaningful to them than anything I might suggest, just as I've learned some of the best sermons are told in front of the fireplace.

---

3 Craddock, *As One Without Authority*, 149.

4. Ibid., 146.

5. Cleave, *Little Bee*, 133–137.

"REQUIREMENTS"

January 30th, 2011
Micah 6:1–8; Matthew 5:1–12

This is a story about a couple named Asa and Hannah who took a vacation to Nigeria. After an uneventful plane ride, the couple had their toes in the sand, walking hand in hand down the beach away from their fancy hotel.

"Listen to that surf, Asa," Hannah said dreamily. "It's so unbelievably *peaceful* here."

In the distance, they heard the sound of a few dogs barking. They paid little attention and were focused instead on the dazzling beauty of the surf. But as the happy couple continued down the white sand, the sound of barking dogs grew closer and closer. Then they heard a rustling in the underbrush along the shoreline.

"What in the world?"

Hannah turned towards the noise and her jaw dropped. Two young African girls emerged from the jungle. They ran straight to Hannah and stood in front of her, clutching each other to keep themselves upright on their trembling legs. One of the girls looked back over her shoulder towards the sound of the barking dogs, but the other stared directly at Hannah.

"Please missus," she said. "Take us to the hotel with you."

It was Asa who answered: "I'm sorry, honey, but the hotel is only for tourists."

"Bad men are hunting us," she replied. "They will kill us if they find us."

At that point, Hannah and Asa could not have known that the village where these children had lived was on top of a major oil reservoir. They did not know that an oil company had hired killers to eliminate the men, women, and children of that village in order to take their land. They did not know that these two young women were the sole survivors and were being pursued in order that the crimes against humanity would remain concealed from the larger world.

Hannah and Asa, however, were immediately aware of the five large dogs that suddenly came crashing out of the jungle. The girls screamed and ducked behind Asa. Just in the nick of time, there was a whistle from behind the dogs. These beasts skidded to a stop, snarling and drooling.

Six men burst forth from the foliage, wielding machetes. Each one had a machine gun slung across his back. They moved past the dogs and right into Asa's face.

Asa gulped and sputtered, "We were just returning to our hotel."

"You will go nowhere," growled one of the men.

Asa spoke with a quivering voice, "We have money, you know!" Failing to get a response, he added hastily, "And we can get more money later!"

"You give me what you got now," the man snarled. "There is no later."

"Asa," whispered Hannah trying to remain calm. "Hand over your wallet!"

Asa reached into his back pocket with shaking fingers and handed over his billfold. Without bothering to count, this man handed the bills to his companions. Hannah breathed a sigh of relief. In response, the man turned and looked directly into her eyes.

"Do you think that you can buy your safety? Money shall not pay for what these girls have seen. These girls must die because of what they have seen. Your money is no good! You will give me these girls."

"No," pleaded Hannah. "Just leave them alone!"

"Hannah," Asa whispered to her out of the side of his mouth. "I think that's the best thing for us to do."

"What, Asa? Are you serious? How do you know they won't kill us too?"

The man apparently overheard their conversation. He turned back to Asa.

"Mister, you want to save these girls?"

Asa coughed and cleared his throat. He wrung his hands and looked around the beach, desperately trying to avoid the man's gaze.

"Well mister, what do you say? Do you want to save these girls?"

It was Hannah who spoke and broke the silence: "Please, sir, if you let us take them back to the hotel, then we will do whatever you want. If you let them come with us, we will give you anything, *anything* you want."

The man laughed bitterly: "You think I care about stuff? You think that your dollars from the rich white world will save these girls?"

Asa finally spoke: "So, what do you want?"

The man raised his right hand and tapped Asa's forehead with his pointer finger.

"You finger, mister. Cut off your finger. You give me your finger and I will give you these girls."

There was a long pause.

"And what if I don't?"

"Then you and your wife will be free to go; but first, you will watch us kill these children."

Hannah looked at the girls still hiding behind her before shifting her gaze to the men and the dogs. Their eyes were on Asa. All waited to see what her husband would do. It seemed that no one was even breathing. They waited to see if Asa could do what was *required*.

Thousands of years before Hannah and Asa went to Nigeria, a Hebrew prophet named Micah asked, "What does the Lord require?" In his initial response to this question, Micah teased his audience with the absurdity of outrageous claims: does the Lord require a thousand rams or ten thousand rivers of oil? These numbers are so huge that they don't even make sense. They are for rhetorical effect.

After Micah played with hyperbole, he turned serious—deadly serious. Shall I come before the Lord, he said, with my firstborn for my transgression, the fruit of my body for the sin of my soul? In other words, does the Lord require human sacrifice? Should you cut off one of your fingers?

Micah gives a resounding "No!" to the question of human sacrifice. In fact, he calls the whole sacrificial system into question. According to this prophet, the Lord requires us to do justice, to love kindness, and to walk humbly with God. Not ten thousand rivers of oil, not a thousand rams, and certainly not the life of another human. It turns out that the Lord requires us to treat one another in certain ways.

But, what exactly is justice and how does one do it? What is kindness and how does one love it? And what in the world does it look like to walk humbly with God? Perhaps these questions depend on the situation that we face.

Hannah and Asa came face to face with a horrible evil, the kind of wickedness that murders children for oil profits. On that beach, sin was as obvious as the hot breath of a deranged killer in their faces. When confronted with this kind of sin, we wish we could pay evil to go away. Asa hands over his wallet and Hannah offers even more money. I imagine that they would have gladly given a thousand rams or even ten thousand rivers of oil. They had money and were willing to give it up.

But evil did not care about their bank account.

So it seems to me that what God requires is actually worth more than money. If we are to do justice, then we cannot abide by injustice. If we are to love kindness, then we must commit to giving ourselves entirely to the cause. If we are walking humbly with God, we are willing to risk it all. True love, Jesus said, lays down its life for another. It is more valuable than anything else.

Back on that beach in Nigeria, Asa took a machete from one of the men and dropped to his knees. He made a fist, but kept one finger extended out on the sand. He closed his eyes and took a deep breath. The machete whipped down through the hot air.

But it sliced only through sand.

When Asa opened his eyes, he saw that the blade had landed far away from his finger. Unable to do what was required, he started sobbing. The men stepped around him in order to grab the girls. Asa had been willing to give up a great amount of money, but he apparently could not meet the requirements of madmen caught up in a depravity that was even bigger than their own sins.

But Hannah dropped to her knees beside her husband. She grabbed the machete that had fallen harmlessly from his hand. She brought the blade down upon her own finger with a perfectly placed *chop*.

Many centuries after Micah preached there came another Hebrew prophet who said, "Blessed are the meek, blessed are the merciful, and blessed are the peacemakers." And if I may be so bold, blessed are the ones who do what is required by sacrificing a part of their very selves. Truly, such sacrifice is love, just as sometimes nine fingers are more than ten.

10

With All Thy Might

THE DEEP WELL OF KNOWLEDGE

DURING MY FIRST YEAR in the parish, I was finishing coursework at the University of Virginia. The masters program, known as Scripture Interpretation and Practice, includes scholars from Judaism, Christianity, and Islam. While I concentrated on early Christian and rabbinic writings, I needed to have one course in Islam in order to complete the degree. So I dutifully made the trip to Charlottesville once a week for several months in the fall of 2010.

After four years of undergraduate and another four years of graduate work, I finally had my first experience in a large lecture hall. For many students, such an atmosphere is a routine part of college, but I had attended small schools and studied subjects that did not have mass appeal—at least, the study of religion used to be specialized. Contrary to my earlier experiences in higher education, I discovered this semester that an introductory course in religion would pack one of the largest classrooms at a state university. As I waited for the first lecture to begin, I overheard snippets of the excited and nervous conversations around me. It became apparent that most students were not studying religion, but sociology, economics, or business. Clearly, Islam is now a major topic across academic disciplines.

Indeed, the diversity of people enrolled in this course reflects the growing role that Islam is playing in our larger culture. When the class began, America was gripped in a controversy surrounding the construction of an Islamic center near Ground Zero of the September 11th attacks in New York City. The role of Islam in American society had become a fixture of national debate.

Dublin is not an area known for diverse religious expression. If you were to visit and take our only exit off the interstate, you would immediately see "Jesus is Lord" proclaimed on a giant billboard. But this billboard does not emphatically speak for all of us. Due primarily to our proximity to several universities, our community is comprised of people with different religious beliefs, including Muslims. In addition, there is diversity among the Christian community, including the ways we view other faiths. That fall, I was fortunate to learn from teachers both in the classroom and in the church.

Ann was one of the first people that I met at New Dublin because she was on the pastoral nominating committee. When she was a young woman, she eloped to the Middle East. For years, she lived as a practicing Muslim in a Muslim country. Now that she has returned to Dublin, she has discovered similarities between Reformed and Islamic theology. Over Arabic coffee in her home, she pointed out that both traditions stress the absolute sovereignty of God. Both traditions claim that one God is the sole ruler of the universe, a deity who is all-powerful and all-knowing, yet all-merciful and all-compassionate. These conversations with Ann stayed with me, and I looked for possible explanations of this commonality during my coursework.

While studying with Professor Ahmed al-Rahim, I learned that Muslims understand their religion as a continuation of the divine revelation to both Jews and Christians. Muhammad believed that his experience of God was not something new, but the same prophetic message given to Moses and Jesus. This belief was likely influenced by historical circumstances. The Arabian Peninsula was located along an important trade route between the Persian and the Holy Roman Empires in the seventh century. Arabian society became aware of Judaism and Christianity through the exchange of merchandise and *ideas* across these land passages. Based on this experience of other cultures and religions, Muhammad may well have been influenced by the Judeo-Christian understanding of monotheism, including such apocalyptic ideas as the resurrection of the dead and the final judgment.[1]

Sadly, this overlap is not often highlighted as Islam becomes more prominent in our larger society. Instead, we are told that Muslims are opposed to other religions, including Christianity and Judaism, even though all three of these traditions trace their roots back to the same

1. Lapidus, *Islamic Societies*, 28–30.

ancestor, Abraham. It is true that the holy scripture of Islam, the Qur'an, includes a few references known collectively as the sword verses. These texts appear to advocate divinely-sanctioned violence against non-Muslims.[2] As is the case with certain Hebrew scriptures like Joshua, the Qur'an was written in a violent era dominated by military campaigns.

But many modern Muslims believe that Judaism and Christianity are genuine revelations from God. They point to passages in the Qur'an that explicitly give special status to Jews and Christians as "people of the book." Professor al-Rahim taught that, according to Islamic theology, God has sent a prophet to every people in order to denounce their particular idolatries and return them to true monotheism. This warning was always the same because God is always the same. Therefore Muslims afford respect to "the people of the book," not only because they believe that Moses and Jesus were prophets, but because the Jewish Torah and Christian gospels were reflections of the original divine message.

Yet Muslims believe that *only* the Qur'an is the pure word of God. The orthodox position maintains that Muhammad simply recited words that came directly from God, spoken to him by the angel Gabriel. In fact, the term, Qur'an, comes from the Arabic word for "recitation." The key point to grasp is that Muslims believe that differences between the Qur'an and other scriptures are the result of tampering by human editors. They argue that we changed our scriptures. Allow me to clarify this seemingly audacious claim.

With respect to the Jews, Muslims point out that the Hebrew Bible is full of anthropomorphic descriptions of the divine.[3] This term, anthropomorphic, describes God with human characteristics, such as God "resting" on the seventh day of creation (Gen 2:2–3). Muslims take issue with the idea that an all-powerful creator would need to rest. The Qur'an states emphatically: "[God] created the heavens and the earth, and all that is between them, in six days, and naught of weariness touched [God]."[4] In fairness, other parts of Hebrew scripture maintain that God does not "slumber nor sleep" (Ps 121:4). Yet anthropomorphisms exist nonetheless, such as when Abraham or Moses seem to talk God out of a decision and even appear to change God's mind (Gen 18:16–33; Exod 32:7–14).

2. Cook, *Muhammad*, 23.

3. Lodahl, *Claiming Abraham*, 50–51.

4. Pickthall, *Qur'an*, 370.

Since the Qur'an is relatively new, especially when compared to the Hebrew Bible, most religious scholars believe that the narratives found in the Qur'an are redactions of the older stories–modifications the material they inherited from the Judeo-Christian tradition. As we see in the example of God resting, the Qur'an retells similar stories by deleting or changing anthropomorphic references so that God does not appear to be human.[5] If it is believed that Muhammad and the early Muslim community were influenced by the Judeo-Christian tradition through cultural exchange along trade routes, then it would follow accordingly that *they* changed our scriptures.

While the argument of "who changed what" is perhaps circuitous, it is interesting to note that anthropomorphism also bothered John Calvin. While he did not compile a different scripture like Muhammad, the Genevan Reformer developed a theory of "accommodation" to explain, for instance, that when Scripture reads that God "repented," this does not mean that God is capable of change. Instead, Calvin argued that the text's description of God was merely put in human terms for human comprehension.[6] In other words, God doesn't really have a change of mind, but we humans certainly do. The Bible is "accommodating" its language to relate to our experience so that we can understand by means of a comparison. With respect to the unchanging nature of God, and yet the anthropomorphic descriptions of certain texts, Calvin had his cake and ate it too.

The Qur'an takes issue with specific Christian beliefs as well. Muslims argue that doctrines concerning the divine nature of Jesus and of the Trinity are human theories that compromise true monotheism.[7] In the Qur'an, there are specific appeals to "the people of the book" to refrain from the belief that Jesus was the Son of God.[8] Granted, we Christians do have some mysterious doctrines! These mysteries are acutely known by anyone who has tried to explain the "math" of three equaling one to young children. In fact, I know many adults who have a hard time believing some of our more miraculous claims. As Ann likes to say, she recites some parts of the Apostles' Creed with her fingers crossed. (I have a hunch that she is not alone in this practice among the

5. Lodahl, *Claiming Abraham*, 11–18.
6. Calvin, *The Institutes*, 226–227.
7. Lodahl, *Claiming Abraham*, 52–56.
8. Pickthall, *Qur'an*, 87–88.

people at New Dublin!) All this is to suggest that many of us have difficulty comprehending the mystery of our own Christian doctrines. We believe in the Trinity, but we ultimately cannot grasp the nature of God, much less explain it.

Calvin recited the Apostles' Creed; yet he was often at pains to contradict his opponents' interpretations of the same doctrines, such as the dual nature of Jesus Christ as both man and God.[9] When arguing with Michael Servetus, for example, Calvin claimed that his interpretation was not new, but rather a return to the original message of Scripture.[10] This is rather like the argument of Islamic theology that the Qur'an reflects the original divine word, which was corrupted by later human misunderstandings. Without overstating the comparison with Calvin, I am intrigued by the idea that Muhammad was more like a reformer at the beginning of his career who sought a return to true monotheism, rather than a new religion.[11] Though Muhammad argued against certain doctrines of Christian theology, his overarching goal was to affirm the prophethood of Jesus without compromising the basic oneness of God. To some degree, this is similar to the Reformers' desire to refrain from throwing the baby out with the bath water in their critique of the Roman Catholic Church. It seems to me that many revolutions are born from an original desire to reform.

Whatever his initial intent, Muhammad's reform movement eventually became a revolution and its own distinct religion. However, my brief discussion points to the tension in the Islamic tradition regarding Judaism and Christianity. On the one hand, Muslims claim that their religion and their revelation are superior. Moses and Jesus are honored by Muslims as prophets, but Muhammad is the *last* prophet. The Jewish Torah and Christian gospel are respected, but the Qur'an is the only true word of God. On the other hand, the Qur'an gives respect and special privileges to believers of other monotheistic faiths, the "people of the book."

Personally, I understand that Muslims would afford a special status to Muhammad and to the Qur'an. After all, Christians honor Jesus and the New Testament. As people of faith, we cannot expect to have authentic engagement with other traditions if we do not bring impor-

9. Calvin, *The Institutes*, 490–491.
10. Calvin, *The Institutes*, 493.
11. Cook, *Muhammad*, 83–89.

tant and cherished beliefs to the conversation table. As Christians, we confess that Jesus is Lord, just as Muslims believe in special prominence of Muhammad. There are unique beliefs to each religion. But as I have indicated, Islam does have much in common with our Judeo-Christian tradition. Learning about these similarities should not gloss over our differences, but a little knowledge can help us to step back and consider the facts objectively. Rather than perceiving Islam as a personal attack on my faith, my education has provided an insight into the development of certain Islamic beliefs. This allows me to think about another religion in nonthreatening ways, and I can engage Muslims colleagues without feeling defensive or compromising my own beliefs. The true value of scholarship is that it can actually build bridges of trust.

While I learned a great deal about Islam at the University of Virginia, I have learned from my experience as a pastor that the importance of scholarship is more than just an academic exercise reserved for a classroom environment. Ann's experience of living in the Middle East with Muslims, Christians, and Jews has led her to search for the fundamental similarities between the three faiths. She says that her bedrock belief is about one God who is the creator and the ruler of all. Ann describes her faith as a deep well: she looks for ways to deepen her reverence for the God of the universe. As I hope to communicate in the rest of this chapter, she has taught me that searching for this deep essence of faith is part of negotiating today's complicated world.

RELIGIOUS RECYCLING

Bud is the only person I've ever known to say, "The Lord has blessed me with scrap metal!" Surrounded by these blessings in his workshop, Bud loves to smoke cigars and tell stories. While he seems happy and content, I've noticed that he often remembers individuals who have tried to deceive him over the years. Perhaps these would-be swindlers learned that appearances can be deceiving because Bud is both intelligent and perceptive. I love the ironic story he tells about the public perception of his chosen profession. When his sons were growing up, mean-spirited children teased them about their father the "junk man." Today he still does the same work, but now he is held in high esteem. With a chuckle, Bud notes that now he is called a *recycler*! In his unique way, Bud speaks to the postmodern idea of truth: perception is just as important as reality.

I am aware that certain Christians and Muslims resist such ideas of relativity; there are movements in both faiths to reclaim the absolute truth of their own religion. But I encounter people in the pews, like Ann, who would like to negotiate a stance between these two opposite extremes of absolute relativity and absolute exclusivity. I studied with another professor at the University of Virginia, Peter Ochs, who refers to a middle ground as "post-liberalism."[12] In a sense, he is recycling philosophy and putting it to another use. Post-liberalism has learned from postmodernity that absolute values must be critiqued. Environmental factors and individual experiences affect our opinions and worldviews. For example, neither a white Christian pastor in Virginia nor a Muslim businessman in Iraq should claim to have a complete grasp of truth because these two people lead very different lives. Yet post-liberalism stresses that very different people can still assert the truth of their own experience. In fact, we must strive to recognize such truths more than ever in a world that is growing increasingly small. We need to work towards shared ideas of wrong and right by listening and learning from one another. If absolute claims are to be avoided, we absolutely must make claims in order to positively affect our world.

I think that post-liberalism negotiates a stance between relativity and exclusivity by moving away from biblical fundamentalism and towards Ann's understanding of faith as a deep well of knowledge. As I understand it, post-liberalism recognizes the uniqueness of different religions, but then asks, what do the New Testament, the Qur'an, and the Hebrew Bible have in common? Physicist Niels Bohr once remarked that the opposite of a profound truth is sometimes another profound truth. Particularly with respect to the Abrahamic traditions, we share fundamental convictions about God that should function as a starting point for conversation. This commonality does not mean that we need to claim or act as if we hold the exact same beliefs; rather our basic convictions should lead us to respectful explorations of our differences. From a starting place of our shared monotheistic convictions, the children of Abraham could then explore the distinctions that make our beliefs personal and alive. Instead of insisting on the absolute nature of one religion, we can speak to the truth of our own faith journey. Instead of shouting at one another, we could listen for all that is good and true and

12. Ochs, "Another Enlightenment," 28–32.

noble and profound. Maybe then the belief that Jesus is Lord could start a conversation, rather than shut one down.

As a part of this interfaith conversation, it seems to me that it is helpful think of different religions as the results of reform movements, just as recyclers make new objects from older materials. Rather than thinking of other faiths as junk, what if we saw others as seeking the same God and putting this knowledge into different forms? Actually, this process should sound familiar for it was modeled for us by the great founders of our monotheistic religions. Moses, Jesus, and Muhammad each had profound beliefs about God that convicted them to speak truth to the power of human rulers and institutions. They believed in their messages so fully that they called for their societies to change. Often bewildered yet committed disciples followed their teachings and spread their messages after their deaths until new communities were formed. In each case, a new religion was believed to be a return to the same God—religious recycling!

I am a follower of Jesus, and I do believe that he is Lord. I also believe that different religions speak truths about God. Undoubtedly, some will disagree with me about this post-liberal view of different religions. Perhaps more of us could simply concur that, just as recycling is good for our environment, cooperation between world religions is good for our societies. By working together, I believe that we can advance peace and justice in our world by respecting one another, including our different religious beliefs. Humbly, I preach to inspire such peacemakers, rather than religious combatants. It is my prayer that all ancestors of Abraham will treat one another as fellow members of the same family. This aim is really just recycling a saying of my Lord, "Blessed are the peacemakers for they will be called children of God" (Matt 5:9).

"A FAITH WELL LIVED"

February 13th, 2011
Deuteronomy 6:4–9; Matthew 5:21–37

There was once a couple who waited and waited and *waited* to have children.[13] Finally, one great and glorious day, a little baby boy was born. He

---

13. The introduction to this sermon is based upon a story E. Carson Brisson, Professor of Biblical Languages at Union Presbyterian Seminary.

was the apple of his father's eye and the song of his mother's heart. As this baby grew, his parents swore to each other that they could actually see him shining in the light of God's love.

Once, when he was just barely three years old, his parents allowed him to stay up past his bedtime. They had, after all, waited years for him and they treasured the extra moments in their hearts. And so, the little boy played happily in front of the fireplace until late in the evening. Gradually, his enthusiasm waned and his eyelids began to droop with the passing of the hours. Determined to stay awake, he marched upstairs in that resolute way of little boys. His favorite train set was in the upstairs playroom and he had his *heart* set upon it. He reached the top of the stairs, but now he was sleepy, so very sleepy that he couldn't even walk! He was a determined *soul*, however, and so he started to crawl across the carpet and down the hall. Finally, just as he reached the doorway, weariness overwhelmed him as he reached for his favorite train with all of his *might*. Right there on the threshold, he fell asleep with his arm outstretched into the playroom.

His mother, who had been watching the whole time, quietly ran and got the camera. She took a single photo without disturbing her sleeping child.

"See," she whispered, "this is a picture of our son's heart and our son's soul."

"And," the father gently added, "it is a picture of all of his might."

What does it mean to love the Lord our God with all of our heart, soul, and might? I believe that the key is found in Jesus' example. Jesus taught, "You have heard that it was said . . . but I say to you . . ." Our Lord was not bound to the literal letter of the law, but interpreted the laws for meaning in his time. Fulfilling the law, Jesus claims, requires us to obey the message at the heart of the law. For example, "do not murder" is one of the Ten Commandments. But Jesus says that the heart of this law is about relationships. Therefore, we must not insult one another. We are to ask for forgiveness. According to Jesus, murder is *any act* that kills a relationship. This interpretation commands us to live as people who practice reconciliation, kindness, and love towards each other. The only way to follow such a law is to live it.

A. J. Jacobs is a writer who committed one year of his life to following every rule in the Bible. That's right, *every rule*, including the ban against shaving the bottom of his beard, the prohibition against wearing clothes that are made out of mixed fibers, and the command to refrain from sitting in the same chair after menstruating women. This last rule proved particularly hard to follow. One time, his wife took out her frustration at her husband's religious antics by walking around their house and sitting in every chair before he got home from work![14]

But finding a seat did not turn out to be Jacobs' real problem.

About midway into his experiment, Jacobs looked the part of an observant Jew, thanks to his beard and sandals, his robe and tassels. One day, he was sitting on a bus reading the book of Ecclesiastes. Suddenly, he felt a tap on his shoulder; he instantly became annoyed because he was reading the Holy Book. Jacobs doggedly continued to read.

"Excuse me," interrupted the man who had tapped his shoulder. Jacobs reluctantly pried his eyes away from Scripture and saw a woman whose face was the color of lima beans.

"This lady is feeling sick," the man continued. Indeed, she was doubled over in pain and had tears streaming down her face.

"Could you give her your seat?"

At that moment, Jacobs realized that, despite his efforts to follow the Bible as literally as possible, he had become what is known in Hebrew as a *Chasid Shote*: a religious idiot.[15]

The attempt to follow the great commands of Scripture should not lead us to become religious idiots. A. J. Jacobs eventually learned how to follow the heart of the law, not by simply reading religious texts, but by listening to that man on the bus who showed him a woman in need right before his eyes. We, too, are fortunate in that we are not alone. Jesus called his disciples together as a community before teaching them the Sermon on the Mount (Matt 5:1). In order to obey the heart of the law, we need each other. No one, no matter how religious or devout, can follow the heart of the law by him or herself. It seems to me that we understand the heart of the law by opening our hearts to others.

Today my heart is turned toward Egypt. The struggle that brought tens of thousands to Tahir Square has ended in *triumph* for freedom! Of course, their work is not done. I realize that there is plenty of uncertainty and anxiety. Democracy could happen, but let's be honest: stability in the

14. Jacobs, *Year of Living Biblically*, 51–52.
15. Jacobs, *Year of Living Biblically*, 118–119.

Middle East could deteriorate and negatively impact the rest of us. At the very least, gas prices rise as political regimes fall.

But isn't our calling to show the love of Jesus to the world by loving those around us? If so, shouldn't we be open to forming relationships with other people, including those who practice different religions? To return to our original question, what does it mean to love the Lord our God with all of our heart, soul, and might?

Just before Hosni Mubarak stepped down as the Egyptian president, tension was high in Tahir Square. Pro-government forces were attacking the protesters and violence was escalating. A large mosque sits in the middle of the square and several thousands of Muslim protesters attended the customary Friday prayer service. Pro-government thugs had made plans to trap the protesters inside while they were praying. However, a group of Egyptian Christians formed a giant circle around the mosque and shielded the Muslims from the attackers. On the following Sunday morning, Muslim protesters formed their own protective circle around a church so that the Christians could worship. Inside the houses of worship, people were praying for protection and for guidance. Outside, people of different religious traditions were an answer to those prayers.

I understand that loving those who are different is difficult, whether we are in Egypt or Virginia; but that is precisely the point. Religious faith is not simply a box to check off in a survey or a duty to perform once a week. We live our faith when we honor God and love our neighbor in all that we do and with all that is in us. Inside this house of worship, we pray for peace and justice. As we go out into the world, may we be an answer to those prayers.

With this goal in mind, perhaps our question becomes what does it *look like* to love the Lord our God with all of our heart, soul, and might? The father who took that picture of his son's heart, soul, and might brought the photograph to work the next day. He framed it and put it in his office, so that he could see his son's outstretched hand from his desk. When he faces weariness or challenges or even tragedies, he looks at that picture. May we, too, be inspired by the example of others to live our faith.

11

Come, Lord Jesus!

ENOUGH IS ENOUGH

Eschatology is the study of the last things. Most people associate the topic with speculations that current events in the world serve as precursors to the second coming of Jesus and the "end times." American culture is saturated with all kinds of these doomsday prophecies, from movies about the year 2012 to billboards that proclaim judgment day. Perhaps most of all, we are influenced by the *Left Behind* books. This theology has penetrated a wide variety of denominations and churches. Even the Methodists in Dublin were reading *Left Behind* in one of their Sunday School classes! But I do not want to sound too judgmental; there were two separate Bible studies about the book of Revelation during my first year at New Dublin. Eschatology seemed to be on everyone's lips. As a result of such interest, I have spent a great amount of time wrestling with this theology. Like Jacob, I hope that we will cling to this topic until we, too, have received a blessing (Gen 32:26).

To begin, I believe this fixation on eschatology is due to the uncertainty and instability in the world. With all of the advances in media technology, we are now aware more than ever of troubling and tragic news, such as global economic problems, revolutions, and famines. While the factors behind these situations are complex, we are allured by the promise of simple answers. Case in point: the *Left Behind* authors seem to "explain" today's disasters by twisting the meaning of certain scriptures into a convoluted yarn that supposedly predicts them. For instance, biblical tribes from the ancient world are believed to represent direct equivalents in modern cultures. This has led some people to claim that the revolt against Hosni Mubarak in Egypt is explained in complete detail by the nineteenth chapter of Isaiah! Not only are such interpretations highly imaginative, they severely distort the plain sense reading of Scripture. Why then are these arguments appealing to so many people?

In addition to the allure of easy answers, I would contend that another part of the popularity of *Left Behind* lies, not in the logic of biblical study, but because these so-called explanations appeal to already held prejudices. Though it seems to take new forms in each generation, the propagation of hateful rhetoric has a sad and long history in the Christian community. Theologians, like Miroslav Volf in his magnificent work *Exclusion and Embrace*, have eloquently shown that many of us reconcile our fear of change and of the unknown by dehumanizing others. During the Reformation, the Papacy was the Antichrist—except, of course, for Roman Catholics who thought the same about the Reformers. White supremacist rhetoric in America has long demonized dark-skinned people. While the Russians represented the evil empire during the Cold War, the same narrative has been all too conveniently applied to Muslims today. By appealing to biases, the *Left Behind* series sets the stage for its popular appeal.

Yet another attractive aspect of *Left Behind* is its unique theology, particular the idea of the rapture. According to this claim, true Christians will be snatched up and taken to heaven before the wrath of God terrorizes the rest of humankind. Bible scholar Elisabeth Schussler Fiorenza has observed that all interpreters maintain "a canon within the canon," meaning that Christians who sincerely believe that they are faithful to the entire biblical witness nonetheless privilege certain texts over others. For the authors of *Left Behind*, 1 Thessalonians 4:13–17 is often cited as the preeminent proof text for the rapture. At this point, I would encourage you to read it for yourself. Does this idea of those who are alive being caught up in the clouds prove the rapture?

Instead of reading a small passage with the teachings of *Left Behind* in mind, we should consider the intention of the actual author. In the context of the entire letter, it is clear that Paul was writing to people who expected the immediate return of Jesus. Indeed, this imminent eschatology is exactly what Paul claims he preached (1 Thess 1:10). The problem, however, was that some members of the Thessalonians' faith community had died, and yet the world was still turning as before (1 Thess 2:14–16). Paul did not want those who were still alive to believe that the deceased had forfeited the promise of eternal life (1 Thess 4:13). The point is that

Paul was distinguishing between the dead and the living: Paul wrote to *encourage* those who had been "left behind," as in those who were still alive (1 Thess 4:18).

With this understanding of the pastoral purpose of 1 Thessalonians, we can now debunk the non-biblical myth of rapture. First of all, it is indisputable that Paul refers to the second coming of Christ in this passage: the image of the Son of Man coming upon the clouds is found in Daniel 7:13, as well as the Synoptic Gospels (Matt 24:30; Mark 13:26; Luke 21:27). But the rapture is not the eschatology that Paul (or any of the other biblical writers) had in mind. In 1 Thessalonians 4:17, the nuance of the "meeting" (Greek *apantesis*) with Christ in the air is analogous to what takes place between an ambassador and city officials. The same Greek word is used in Acts 28:15 to describe a delegation from Rome who went out to "meet" Paul and his companions. The point is that the delegation welcomed the travelers and then *returned* to the city with them. This is completely opposite of the rapture's idea in which people are whisked away from earth.

This rapture theology popularized by *Left Behind* is a misinterpretation of the Bible, which is partially the reason why it has only been around for about a hundred years. But the idea of the rapture is popular because it relates perfectly to our modern society's self-understanding as a destined group of individuals marked for greatness. Complicated world events are neatly "explained" as necessary precursors to the salvation of certain chosen people. Like a golden parachute, true believers will be raptured before the wrath of heaven destroys those other doomed people. Isn't it telling that the rapture happens at the very beginning of the first book, yet the *Left Behind* series continues for thousands of pages? It seems to me that their rapture is akin to the promise of a heavenly pay-per-view event, during which you can watch God punish people you hate from a front row seat in heaven. While you wait for your ticket, you can read about it in the meantime!

I realize that this last statement is particularly harsh and accusatory. Perhaps a dose of humility is in order: I will admit that my analysis of the *Left Behind* movement also reflects my own cultural biases. If rapture proponents want other people to be punished, I would like for us to all get along. My view also reflects my social location. I have a privileged life and, quite frankly, I want it to continue. If I am honest, I do not want the world the end because I look forward to the future and make plans. I want to raise children and write books, continue to serve at New Dublin and travel to new places. I do not believe that there is anything wrong with these goals, yet I recognize that I bring such an agenda to my interpretation of the Bible. I, too, have a favored canon within the biblical canon. While the *Left Behind* authors advance a radically different agenda, we are equally guilty of bringing our own opinions to the text. Indeed, how could we not? We are humans who interact with Scripture through our own experiences and worldviews.

With this recognition, we need to broaden our interpretations by considering different viewpoints, especially from people outside our daily experience. Rather than dismissing eschatology because it has been corrupted in my own culture, I remember the vast majority of people in today's global economy who do not live with the same privileges that I enjoy. While I maintain my critiques of distorted readings of Scripture and flawed understandings of theology, I understand that the end of this world as we know it is appealing to those who suffer from poverty, disease, war, racism, and imperialism. Many people live on less than a dollar a day and under the real threat of death. It is easy to imagine that such communities would yearn for an end to the pain and struggle that they experience on a regular basis. These are the people whose hearts join in crying out the ancient refrain, "Come, Lord Jesus!" (Rev 22:20).

One of Anne Lamott's novels describes a mother who came across an acronym for *love*: "Letting Others Voluntarily Evolve." At first, this sounds great; but what if the person you love is making bad choices? Voluntary evolution and other forms of self-improvement are wonderful, but surely, Lamott's character reasons, there is a time and a place for a loving parent to step in and say, "Enough is enough!"[1] At precisely this point, eschatology becomes a loving rescue for those who are suffering, as opposed to a disastrous punishment for those "left behind."

There is a Catholic priest in Guatemala who once summarized the civil war that ripped apart his nation for thirty-six years: "An evangelical pastor who became military dictator directed one of the most horrifying campaigns of violence, invoking the name of God to justify waging a campaign of genocide against the rural Mayan population. [Guatemala] is a country so astoundingly gripped by greed and corruption that a mere two percent of the population owns some ninety-eight percent of the wealth. Children routinely die of diseases that were probably curable

1. Lamott, *Imperfect Birds*, 158.

even in the time of Jesus."[2] It is only if we can imagine this brutal and tragic context that we might truly make sense of this priest's eschatology. When asked what he thought Guatemala most needed, he said, "For Jesus Christ to come back to earth and teach people how to act better."[3] Notice that he does not want to be raptured away! I think it is to his credit that his call for Christ's return is *instructive*, rather than vindictive. He wants his enemies to learn the error of their ways, rather than receive punishment for the atrocities they perpetrated. Yet I hear his eschatological hope loud and clear: he wants God to step in and say, "Enough is enough!"

I recognize that I live a comfortable life; however I am motivated to make the world around me a better place. Through Scripture, church tradition, and personal experience, God is teaching me "how to act better," and I want to teach others to do the same. Therefore, *discipleship* is important to any discussion of eschatology. I believe that living in accordance to the idea that God will one day right all wrongs should inspire us to help those who are suffering right now. Rather than living with anxiety and fear, we can strive to follow the example of the one who gave his life in order that others might truly live. Gandhi put it like this: be the change you want to see in the world. In Christian terms, we say that we are called to be the hands and feet of Christ on earth. If we practiced this belief more consistently, Gandhi might not have said that he liked our Christ but not our Christians.

While I have argued that the *Left Behind* series is a distortion of the doctrine of eschatology, I admit that there is a limit to my own way of thinking, which emphasizes the role of discipleship. Critics would label my view as an over-realized eschatology. In trying to be the hands and feet of Jesus on earth, some argue that such theology glorifies the church rather than the Son, thereby replacing divine power with human power. It seems to be true that theologians in mainline denominations have tended to downplay the importance of eschatology, the study of last things, in favor of the role of ecclesiology, the study of the church. Many nineteenth-century theologians believed that the church would eventually conquer evil with good in all parts of the world. While the Christian faith has spread across the globe, the twentieth century was the most violent era of human history. Sadly, the new millennium contin-

---

2. Goldman, "The Gospel According to Matthew," 210.
3. Goldman, "The Gospel According to Matthew," 211.

ues this horrific pattern of human behavior. Perhaps the greatest of the nineteenth-century theologians, Friedrich Schleiermacher, spoke of the doctrine of the return of Christ as "the consummation of the Church," but he insisted that this would only be possible through a "sudden leap to perfection" as "an act of Christ's kingly power."[4] Even at its very best, the church needs God's help.

So it seems that the Guatemalan priest is correct. If we are going to act better, we need Jesus to come back and teach us. Try as we might, we humans are never going to bring about true peace on earth. With this point, we realize that humankind is in need of a savior. We need to be rescued by someone or something beyond our control because, left to our own devices, we have consistently made a mess of our world at the expense of others. This is the standard confession of the Reformed faith: just as we are saved by grace alone, our world must ultimately be redeemed by divine intervention. On a basic level, I can agree with Christians from all denominations who believe that our society will reach a point in which only God can say, "Enough is enough!"

However, it seems to me that the real question concerns our actions in the meantime. While we must guard against putting our faith solely in the church, I maintain that the ethics of eschatology are ultimately about discipleship: How can we live as disciples while believing that our Lord will come again? Are we going to propagate a culture of fear that demonizes others or a culture of compassion that reaches out to those in need?

THE FACE OF HOPE

My grandmother once heard a hellfire and brimstone pastor making doomsday predictions on a Christian radio program. At first, I actually thought that Gran was napping in the front seat of the car, blissfully unaware of the propaganda spewing across the airwaves. Suddenly, she sat up straight and declared, "Well he has his opinion, but I choose to be hopeful!"

Like my grandmother, I am firmly convinced of the power of hope. I would like to point out that she and I are not alone in this conviction. Jesus repeatedly admonishes his followers, "Be not afraid" (Matt 10:31, 14:27, 17:7, 28:10). For Paul, our greatest hope is that God will

---

4. Schleiermacher, *The Christian Faith*, 708.

recreate the world. All of creation yearns for the coming glory of Christ as a woman in labor pains (Rom 8:18–20). Paul also describes Christ's resurrection from the dead as the "first fruits," meaning that, since God first raised Jesus from the dead, we also will be resurrected at the return of Christ (Rom 8:18–25; 1 Cor 15:20–24). Notice that there is no mention of rapture. Paul's images are arresting as much for their simplicity as their promise: what God began on the cross, God will complete in the second coming. Our hope is that God has such power.

We should also bear this hope in mind whenever we hear supposed predictions about the end times. Jesus said that not even the Son of Man knows when the end will come (Matt 24:36; Mark 13:32). Likewise, Paul never attempted to set a fixed date for the second coming. Rather than reading the "signs of the times" to predict the future or prepare for the rapture, Paul's method was to inspire ethical living for the present because of what God did through Jesus Christ in the past. Simply put, God's gift of grace in Jesus Christ exhorts us to action! The reality of human shortcomings should not prevent us from working for good in our world. As Paul famously said, we do not sin in order than grace might abound (Rom 6:1). Instead he claimed that Christ died so that we might live no longer for ourselves, but for Christ (2 Cor 5:15). These verses clearly understand the Christian faith as a commitment to work for good in the world, unlike the writings of certain authors that contend the true believers will somehow be whisked away. Since God so loved the world that he gave his only begotten son, we should love each other in response.

I received a phone call from one of my parishioners late one evening. He was in near hysterics. He kept repeating that his loved one was "cooling her heels in jail." The details of the story were hazy (and need not be rehearsed here), but we did take a lot of deep breaths together over the phone. Then I went to visit him and we prayed for his loved one together. As I was taught in seminary, I tried to be a relatively non-anxious presence and listen attentively. But nothing I said or did had any noticeable effect—that is, until my parishioner suggested that I make a visit to the jail. Though this idea gave him some comfort, now I was the one who needed to take deep breaths!

The first time I made this visit, the young woman "cooling her heels" was a physical and emotional train wreck. She cried throughout our conversation. Her hair was a long and tangled mess, dirty and stringy.

Loose strands fell across her forehead and mixed with her tears, clinging to the wetness on her cheeks. I correlated the disarray of her hair to the rest of her life situation.

When I returned a few days later, I almost couldn't believe my eyes. There she sat, collected and in control, speaking calmly to me from the other side of the protective glass. Her hair was washed and combed, pulled back from her face in a neat ponytail. It seemed to me that she had somehow tied her hopes back together as well. Incredulously, I asked her what had changed. What has made such a difference in your life?

During her first few days in jail, she was unable to speak to anyone and just wanted to be left alone. She desperately wanted to sleep and thereby escape her situation, but she tossed and turned, tormented by her worries and regrets. A sleepless wreck, she slowly began to share her situation with others around her. She was surprised to learn that other prisoners had their own sad tales, some of which were even more tragic than her own. While in prison, she experienced real support by reaching out to others and discovering that they were reaching out to her. She laughed and sheepishly admitted that one of her new found confidants had even volunteered to tidy up her hair!

I do not wish to romanticize jail. This young woman was quick to point out the horrors of incarceration, including the fear of other women who were unrepentant of their violent crimes. I also do not wish to portray myself as some kind of heroic bearer of the gospel. In fact, she especially wanted yours truly to know that she was an atheist. She did not think that God had anything to do with her situation. I did not "convert" her anymore than I busted her out of prison; I did get a new insight to the mandate of Jesus to visit those in jail.

According to the eschatology of a famous parable in the Gospel of Matthew, we will be judged, not by our profession of faith but by our actions, specifically by our willingness to be among those who are suffering. At the end of time before the judgment seat, what matters is whatever you do for the least of these (Matt 25:31–46). Justification by faith alone is a central tenant of Reformed theology; yet it seems that works matter.

My friend and mentor, Carla Pratt Keyes, once told the following joke in one of her sermons. The story goes that a Presbyterian clergyman died and went to Peter at the gates of heaven. The pastor confidently told Peter his name and the saint checked his list.

"Ah yes, a Presbyterian pastor of forty-five years—you go straight to hell!"

Utterly dejected and forlorn, the pastor found his way to the entrance of the fiery furnace. Much to his surprise, he saw none other than the great leaders of the Protestant Reformation, Martin Luther and John Calvin, sitting amongst the flames with their heads bowed in shame. The pastor rushed up to Calvin:

"John, how can it be that you and I are here and not in heaven?"

Calvin slowly shook his head in disgust: "Well, it turns out that works *do matter*."

Humor aside, we do need to get to work. As Rob Bell wrote, "Jesus passionately urges us to live like the end is here, now, today."[5] Disciples are called to visit people in their distress. Rather than seeking an escape from the suffering in the world, we need to pray with those who are grieving, visit those in prison, feed the hungry, clothe the naked, and share our stories. Like the righteous people in Jesus' parable who discovered they were helping the Lord when they helped the needy, we might just surprise ourselves by the eternal consequences of our actions. Sometimes the face of hope has a nice, neat ponytail.

Maybe the "end times" are just around the corner. It could quite literally end for anyone of us at any point, so we need to be in touch with our own mortality. In the Christian year, Lent is a sacred time to experience God in profound ways, perhaps through fasting and meditating on the mortality of creaturely existence, or maybe through pushing out of comfort zones and reaching out a hand to those who need help. To live in this way is to blend discipleship with eschatology.

While there is much about the deep mysteries of eschatology that I do not understand, I believe that our greatest hope is that God will bring about the new heaven and the new earth (Rev 21:1–5). As we wait, we recognize that the same God who will recreate existence places a dramatic calling on us in today's world. As disciples, we should live like the end is here. We are to serve, rather than be served—to be with those who are suffering, rather than to seek an escape for ourselves. Until the time when God will dry every tear from every eye, we must see the tears of our neighbor as our call to action. We must be a face of hope to someone in need until that day when, as Julian of Norwich said, all shall be well and all manner of things shall be well.

5. Bell, *Love Wins*, 197.

"CROSS TOGETHER"

Ash Wednesday; March 9th, 2011
Joel 2:1–17, 2 Corinthians 5:20—6:11

Eugene Peterson is a terrific scholar and author of *The Message* translation of the Bible. But when he was a little boy, he just wanted to be a butcher like his father. His father wore a white apron and so Eugene wore one too. His mother made him a smaller version out of flour sacks. With every inch he grew, she made a new one that was just a little bit bigger until he was large enough to fit into one of his father's aprons.[6]

It seems to me that this image of growing into larger aprons is a fitting metaphor for the journey that we call Lent. As part of the observance of this liturgical season, there are many ways to grow spiritually: some give up caffeine, others give up chocolate. Like putting on a new piece of clothing, you can also add a spiritual discipline, such as reading the Bible for twenty minutes in the morning. All of these practices are great ways to grow in faith, inch by inch and day by day.

Yet Lent also points to something larger than just ourselves and our personal spiritual journeys. Just as Jesus set his face towards Jerusalem for his death and resurrection, Lent points to the cosmic drama that is progressing in human history. Our world moves towards a certain end that the Hebrew prophets refer to as the great and fearful Day of the Lord. In our passage from Joel this evening, we read about fantastic images of war and fire, the earth quaking and the heavens trembling, the sun and the moon and even the stars turning to darkness. With these fantastic and terrifying images in mind, it is easy to let our imaginations run wild.

You might recall a children's story about Henny Penny, also known as Chicken Little, who has an acorn fall on his head. Due to his interpretation of his own personal experience, he comes to the conclusion that, "The sky is falling! The sky is falling!" And so, he runs around, spreading hysteria and paranoia. This is a fable, but truth can be stranger than fiction.

In the nineteenth century, there was a pastor named John Nelson Darby who nearly died from a disease. For all intents and purposes, he took this personal experience and invented a story about the sky fall-

6. Peterson, "My father's butcher shop," 28.

ing. Darby's tale proved to be convincing, in large part, because he had a highly selective way of reading the Bible, cherry-picking verses out of their context and stringing them together.[7] You may not have heard of John Nelson Darby, but I bet you've heard of the *Left Behind* series. The authors, Tim LaHaye and Jerry Jenkins, have taken Darby's theory about the falling sky and produced books, movies, and video games about something called the rapture. If the sales of this merchandise are any indicator, there are millions of people who have bought into the idea that some will be "left behind."

Tonight, I want to make it clear that the church existed for nearly two thousand years without this theology; furthermore, the word "rapture" never appears in all of Scripture. The rapture may be popular, but it is not biblical. As scholar Barbara Rossing wrote, "The version of Christ's second coming publicized by Rapture proponents—a one-two punch with an invented seven-year period of violence—is not based on scripture or the way Christian tradition presents the coming of Jesus."[8] Such distortions of Scripture and theology do not lead to spiritual growth during Lent or any other time of year.

But let me be just as clear that Scripture and Christian tradition do teach about the second coming of Jesus. One of the oldest Christian beliefs is that Jesus will return again. As we recite in the Apostles' Creed, "[Jesus] sitteth on the right hand of God the Father, from thence he shall come to judge the quick and dead." We must realize, however, that the second coming is *not* the rapture. The great and terrible Day of the Lord is about cosmic disorder, but it remains a message of *hope*—the destruction that is prophesized is only the prelude to new life. Like an old butcher's apron must be discarded in order to put on the new one, so Paul says that if anyone is in Christ, there is a new creation: everything old has passed away and everything has become new (2 Cor 5:17). Inch by inch and day by day, God is moving human history towards its final culmination. Hear these beautiful words from Revelation: "I saw a new heaven and a new earth; for the first heaven and the first earth had passed away, and the sea was no more. And I saw the holy city, the new Jerusalem, coming down out of heaven from God, prepared as a bride adorned for her husband. And I heard a loud voice from the throne saying, 'See, the home of God is among mortals. He will dwell with them;

7. Rossing, "The So-Called Rapture," 81.
8. Ibid.

they will be his peoples, and God himself will be with them; he will wipe every tear from their eyes'" (Rev 21:1–4).

My friends, these are words of hope. At the most basic level, it seems to me that we must resist the rapture theology because it fails to emphasize the biblical hope: we trust for our future because of what God has done in the past. We must believe that the future is in the hands of the same God who died for us. The rapture is about escaping from the world, yet Jesus came to earth to suffer with us in order to save us. If we begin with what Jesus did for us on the cross, I think that we will discover a way to live in the world as Jesus lived. My friends, no one is left behind; we are on a spiritual journey together.

In her memoir, Elizabeth Gilbert documents her year of living in Italy, India, and Indonesia. She selected Italy as one of her destinations because she hoped to learn Italian. As she studied the language, she discovered her favorite Italian word, *attraversiamo*, which means, "Let's cross over together." You say *attraversiamo* to a friend, as a sign of support. Gilbert loved this word so much that she would drag a friend back and forth across a busy street, shouting "*Attraversiamo!* Let's cross over together!"[9] People thought she was strange, but I understand Gilbert's affinity for the word. It is good to have someone who is with us every step of the journey.

In a similar way, Christians should try to cross over with one another, rather than believe that some of us will be "raptured" away. When Paul says that we are "ambassadors for Christ" (2 Cor 5:20), he is encouraging us to walk together. As ambassadors, we go ahead of Christ and tell others about our hope for the future. As ambassadors, we declare that new life is rising from the ashes because God's love is greater than sin and even death. While we cannot always be sure of what is going on in the world around us, *attraversiamo*—whatever we face in the road ahead, let us walk through it together.

In just a moment, we will have the opportunity to receive ashes on our foreheads in the sign of the cross. This serves as a reminder that we are made of dust and we will return to dust. Tonight, we participate in this ancient ritual as a community. With the sign of the cross, we pledge to cross over together. No one should be left behind; we are here to encourage one another with the good news: Christ has died, Christ has risen, Christ will come again.

9. Gilbert, *Eat, Pray, Love*, 71–72.

Fellow ambassadors, we look for the great and fearful day of the Lord with hope. May this season of Lent be a time for growing into this grace, inch by inch and day by day. Whether we give up old practices or add new habits, *attraversiamo*! May we bear our crosses together until Jesus comes again.

12

Runaway Bulls

THE HOUSE THAT CALVIN BUILT

JOHN CALVIN, THE FATHER of Reformed theology, had a prolific writing career. He wrote a commentary on every book of the Bible except Revelation. His magnum opus, *Institutes of the Christian Religion*, was a lifelong work in progress and eventually expanded well over a thousand pages. Calvin was also preacher, and the pages that have survived from his sermons rival even his academic works. But despite this abundance of incredibly diverse material, most people associate Calvin with only one doctrine: predestination. Ironically, it is this aspect of his theology that is the least understood.

The idea of predestination strikes people as unfair. How can our future be determined by an all-powerful being without any input from us? I will readily grant that some forms of predestination are downright awful, including the idea that God condemns people to hell before they were even born. Does the idea of predestination mean that God is like a cosmic puppeteer? How can we worship a God like that?

These are good questions to ask. As I endeavored to show in the previous chapter, we must challenge distorted readings of Scripture and flawed theology. But while I want to put predestination under a microscope, we should try to analyze the concept from Calvin's point of a view. As a systematic theologian, Calvin did not formulate his controversial beliefs flippantly. We can think of the construction of his theology like the building of a house: he laid the foundation first and then added other parts to the main structure.

Calvin began with the understanding of God's absolute omniscience or all-knowing. Everything has always been and will always be known to God. Calvin reasoned that, in order to have complete knowledge of the entire scope of human history, God must be outside of time. In his words, "nothing is future or past, but all things are present."[1] According to Calvin, predestination cannot be thought of as "seeing into the future" because such a concept of time does not exist for God. By contrast, humans are in time and, consequently, we understand reality in sequential terms, as a movement from one thing to the next. This insight is remarkable in that it anticipates the scientific claims about general relativity in the twentieth century.

Perhaps we can better understand this complex idea through a comparison to our experience. The classic American Protestant conversion story is a heartfelt declaration of Jesus as savior. In John Wesley's memorable terminology, one moment we are afraid, but then our heart becomes "strangely warm" and we are changed. For God, however, the future is held together with the past and present in one divine reality. God could not experience this conversion as a series of events because God does not have to wait to see what will happen next! From God's perspective, a moment in our time is both an instant and an eternity.

In addition to God's omniscience, God's omnipotence or all-powerfulness was another foundational aspect of Calvin's theology. Jesus said, "For mortals it is impossible, but for God all things are possible" (Matt 19:26). Interestingly, this statement about God's omnipotence was prompted by the disciples' urgent question, "Who can be saved?" (Matt 19:25). For Calvin and other Reformed theologians, a central tenant of faith was that human salvation is only by the grace of God. Calvin summarized, "To make it clear that our salvation comes about solely from God's mere generosity, we must be called back to the course of election."[2] We do not choose God anymore than we "have" faith; we are chosen by God and given faith. The concept of Jesus as savior necessarily means that we cannot save ourselves. Therefore we are completely reliant upon God; for all things are possible for God.

While many Protestants profess such beliefs in God's omnipotence, most do not consider this grace in light of God's omniscience. If salvation is a gift from God, then surely God knows about this plan. And if God's knowledge is outside of time, then God knows the fate of everyone, at all times, all at once! By arranging his argument in this

1. Calvin, *Institutes*, 926.
2. Ibid., 921.

fashion, I am suggesting that Calvin reasoned backwards to predestination. Predestination was not the focal point of his systematic theology, but a consequence of holding together different attributes of God. To press the metaphor further, predestination was like an area rug: it was laid on top of the theological foundation. Or perhaps predestination is like a skylight: it shined light on the nature of God, but it was not part of the main structure.

LIVING THE QUESTIONS

While I enjoy such abstract speculation, theology is never written in a vacuum. As is true for us, Calvin's thoughts about God were based on his experience in the world. One of my theology professors at Union Presbyterian Seminary, Dawn Devries, once told me that Calvin saw a runaway bull break through a fence, tear through a field, and gorge several people to death. The violence of the event shocked him. In the *Institutes*, he catalogues a long list of potentially dangerous activities and situations before concluding, "Now, wherever you turn, all things around you not only are hardly to be trusted but almost openly menace, and seem to threaten immediate death."[3] It is a scary world out there!

Regardless of one's opinion about Calvin, we must wrestle with the "runaway bulls" of our own time. We are fully aware of disasters on a global scale. In March of 2011, a terrible earthquake and tsunami decimated Japan. This tragedy came on the heels of the devastating earthquake in Haiti from a year ago. We cannot deny the theological questions raised by horrific physical suffering and losses of life. Why do natural disasters devastate communities? How could a loving God allow such suffering? Where is God?

Though appreciative of much of his sophisticated theology, I admit that Calvin was not always helpful with regard to these thorny questions. He wrote, "In times of adversity, believers comfort themselves with the solace that they suffer nothing except by God's ordinance and command."[4] Calvin's most terrifying thought was that such violence could happen at *random*. But should we believe that God ordained and commanded tragedies and suffering? Do we really think that a God of

3. Ibid., 223.
4. Ibid., 200.

love, mercy, and compassion would bury people alive under tons of concrete?

No! Absolutely not!

Before we attempt to make claims about who God is, it is just as important to stress who God is *not*. God is not a cosmic sadist or matador of runaway bulls. As William Sloane Coffin has rightly preached, "God doesn't go around this world with his finger on triggers, his fist around knives, his hands on steering wheels."[5]

So then, what do we do with tragedy? Do we simply say that God was not involved at all? The Deists of the American Enlightenment believed that God is the clockmaker who created the world and now allows the machine to run according to its own laws. As Christians, we agree with the idea that God is creator. However, we assert that God is decidedly *hands on*. Jesus is God in the flesh, the God who became human (Phil 2:5–8). Therefore, the Creator is also deeply and personally involved with all of creation. Rather than questioning God's involvement, it seems to me that we need to consider the nature of God's involvement, the crux of the matter: *How* is God involved in our world?

In his powerful sermon after his son's death, Coffin preached that God's heart is the first of all our hearts to break when tragedy occurs.[6] I think that Coffin could make such a claim because God became human in the person of Jesus Christ. While Calvin built upon a foundation of God's omniscience and omnipotence, I think that we need to keep the incarnation in mind when we try to understand God's involvement in the world. As one of us, God suffers with us. The nature of God's involvement with humankind may be summarized by the incredible claim that Emmanuel—God with us—is Christ crucified. If this is who God is, then we can trust God. We can trust in God's "compassion," literally that God is "with our passions"—our struggles, our tears, and our runaway bulls. What else could be the message of the cross? God's involvement with the world does not mean that evil will not occur; it means that life will come from death.

Out of the horrible tragedy of Japan's earthquake and tsunami, I trust that God's involvement is glimpsed in the following story. There was a Japanese recovery crew who, amidst the rubble of destruction, heard the faintest whimper. These men looked at each other in disbelief: did we

5. Coffin, "Alex's Death," 263–264.

6. Ibid., 264.

really just hear a baby cry? Out here in all this death and destruction, did we really hear the sound of life? One of the crew members bent down into the rubble of a house, lifted broken planks and pushed aside cracked bricks. And there, like a flower pushing up from an ashtray of cigarette butts, was a tiny baby, safe and sound, wrapped in a pink blanket.

Happy endings, of course, always lend themselves to preaching more readily than open-ended questions. But our faith is built on trust and not upon answers. Sometimes we simply must say that we do not understand the mysterious ways of God. While Calvin often made this point, the great poet, Rainer Maria Rilke, perhaps puts it best in his *Letters to a Young Poet*: "Try to love the questions themselves, like locked rooms and like books written in a foreign language. Do not now look for the answers. They cannot now be given to you because you could not live them. It is a question of experiencing everything. At present you need to live the question."[7]

When tragedy strikes, when people die too young, or when bulls run loose, there is much we cannot know or say. But I do believe that we must first claim that God is not the cause of tragedy: God is love (1 John 4:8). In making such a claim, we do well to follow Rilke and think of this statement of faith in terms of questions: how is God love? Where is God's love in our world? How can we show God's love to others? As we live into these profound questions, we take comfort knowing that God experiences pain with us as the Incarnate God who entered our world as a human being. As disciples of the God who became flesh, we should therefore offer comfort to each other: "Beloved, let us love one another, because love is from God" (1 John 4:7). The question about the nature of God's involvement becomes directed at us: How are we involved with those who are in need?

OUT OF CHAOS, HOPE

On April 8th, 2011 the town of Pulaski suffered the first tornado ever recorded in the county. Thankfully, there were no casualties; but high winds decimated roughly fifty homes and left approximately four hundred people in need of shelter. Even worse, the damage occurred to low-income residences, many of which lacked insurance.

---

7. Rilke, *Letters*, 35.

New Dublin responded immediately by hosting a variety show fundraiser. All of the proceeds went to the Red Cross Emergency Response Team, which had set up shelters in the affected areas. On the night of the event, our youth served lasagna and homemade desserts. Then people of all ages got up on stage to showcase their talent, including jokes, music, and the creation of crafts made exclusively out of duct tape! As we cheered each performer, my heart was full for the families in need of help and for our members who needed to help.

The following Sunday, I arranged several dozen tea candles on the Lord's Table. Before we celebrated Holy Communion, I invited the congregation to light a candle as a prayer for someone in their family, our community, or anyone in our world. As individuals came forward, we all sang a Taize song. I was playing guitar just off to the side and focusing on the music. Gradually, I became aware of a problem: some of our members were taking a very long time to light just one candle. They were unable to use the lighters because of the safety lock. So we sang and sang and *sang*. The Taize song is repetitive by nature, but we took it to a new level!

When I finally put down my guitar in order to preside over the sacrament, I paused to look at the candles. Despite all of that time and effort, many candles remained unlit. I could only smile to myself. We are called to be light the world; yet it is also true that some of our efforts seem futile. We try and try and *try*, but at the end of the day, some things just will not ignite. As we gather around the Lord's Table, we do not deny these frustrations or failures. We point to the free gift of God—the light that shines in the darkness. This does not mean that things will be easy or that we will be able to explain everything that happens. Rather, we remember the life, death, and resurrection of Jesus in whom the light shone for all to see, even on the darkest day. Because all things are possible for God, God can work through anything and inspire everyone. Our efforts are never wasted. It is our faith, not our work, which illuminates our experience. And so, we gamely sing on with lit and unlit candles, trusting that all things are possible with God.

In the months after the tornado, our church led the effort to assist a family who had lost their home. It was not always easy to coordinate with county officials or other volunteers from churches all across the state. But we had Dave. Only a few months before, he became an elder for the first time. When the disaster occurred, our session encouraged

Dave to get involved with the Presbyterian Disaster Assistance. He was the perfect choice due to his extensive training as a general contractor and background in construction. In addition, he proved to be an invaluable leader and committed worker. When he thanked our volunteers as part of Sunday worship, Dave said that Paul's words truly spoke to him: "By the grace of God I am what I am" (1 Cor 15:10). It is grace to be the right person who is ready and willing to serve in the right capacity. Under Dave's leadership and spiritual vision, we responded to the tragedy of the tornado by building a house. In partnership with other churches and volunteers, we lived into the motto of the Presbyterian Disaster Assistance: out of chaos, hope.

I do not know why a tornado hit our community or why the bulls get loose. I do not know why newborns die in hospitals or why foreign bombs kill children in schools. But neither can I explain how people of all ages would work together in order to lend a helping hand. I can't explain how an individual (dare we say!) is *predestined* to work on behalf of those in need. What I do know is that I am inspired by such people. I am encouraged by their witness to God's love through their love for others. And so, I can stand in the pulpit on Sunday mornings and proclaim the questions for us to live.

TESTS OF FAITH

April 10th, 2011
Genesis 22:1–14

I recently heard the tragic tale of a father who had lost his one-year-old daughter to cancer. How could anyone describe such pain? Words simply fail to convey the depth of sorrow and lament.

Though this grieving father could not express his loss, he did have some particularly choice words for God. How could a loving God allow this to happen? Where was God? When his family tried to comfort him, he angrily denounced their religion. What is the point in having faith when so much suffering is in the world? How could anyone believe?

As a pastor, his pain and anger grieve me. They also leave me groping for the right words to say in response. When I was a hospital chaplain, a different father who had just lost his only child pointed his finger directly into my chest and shouted, "*Your* God did this to *my* child!"

What does it mean to talk about a God of love when tragedy strikes? What does it mean to believe that God is generous and good when someone's baby dies?

One answer handed down through Christian history is that suffering is ennobling. It builds character. I think that this is true—up to a point. In high school, I broke my index finger on my left hand halfway through baseball season. For weeks, every time I caught the ball in my glove, my finger stabbed with pain. This was particularly problematic because I was a catcher and caught literally hundreds of pitches a day! But the pain made me tougher. It also focused my concentration.

I offer this illustration as a metaphor for suffering that is ennobling. I think that a particular passage from James suggests this interpretation: "My brothers and sisters, whenever you face trials of any kind, consider it nothing but joy, because you know that the testing of your faith produces endurance; and let endurance have its full effect, so that you may be mature and complete, lacking in nothing" (Jas 1:2–4). Those are strong and inspiring words of faith.

But let's be honest: there are more difficult trials in life than broken fingers. Only certain people seem to have been dealt the most difficult hands. The tornado destroys only a few houses in only certain parts of town. The brain tumor develops in only a small percentage of infants.

For the people who are directly affected, such tragedies are only made worse by attempts to explain them. I think that it would be nothing short of *abusive* to quote that passage in James to the father who has just lost his child. In fact, the father who lashes out at religion is most likely reacting to some form of this abusive theology, railing against some possibly well-meaning person who has told him that "what doesn't kill him will only make him stronger." We should avoid giving easy answers to difficult questions because there may come a time when no answers can explain loss, pain, or God.

If this is true, then what in the world are we supposed to do with this difficult story we've just read about Abraham and Isaac?

Supposedly, Mark Twain once remarked that is wasn't the passages in the Bible that he didn't understand that bothered him. He was bothered by the texts that he *did* understand. Our text today should bother us. The story concerns the idea of child sacrifice as an act of worship or as a sign of obedience to God. As Bible scholars have pointed out, this story reflects a moral struggle that was being negotiated in the original, historical community. There is evidence that ancient cultures, perhaps even the Israelites, practiced forms of child sacrifice. However, the prophet Jeremiah unequivocally condemns this practice (Jer 19:5). How could the same God command Abraham to slaughter Isaac and yet forbid child sacrifice through the voice of the later prophets? Did God change God's mind?

It seems to me that it is our understandings *about* God that change. Theologian J. B. Phillips tells the story of teenagers in the 1950s who didn't believe that God could understand the sonar radar.[8] They thought of God as some old man in the sky with antiquated views. With the same flawed reasoning, today's generation might not think that God could operate Facebook! It is a valid point to note that some of our human perceptions of God change over time. Just because we advance as a society, either technologically or morally, this does not mean that God needs to catch up.

But, as I suggested at the beginning, there is more at stake than just abstract musings about the nature of God. There are some questions that are utterly *timeless*. What does it mean to talk about a God of love when tragedy strikes? What does it mean to believe that God is generous and good when someone's baby dies?

As I struggled with these questions in light of our text from Genesis, my attention was drawn to the two servants whom Abraham brings along for the journey. Some would say that these two characters are merely included as an afterthought. But I wonder if we are most like these two servants. At least, I see a reflection of my own story in theirs. I am not a hero of the faith like Abraham nor am I a victim like Isaac. I've never heard the voice of God nor faced a deadly situation. However, I have been in the presence of many people who were in crisis. Many of these crises had to do with beliefs about God and what God expected from them, like the grieving father, jamming his finger in my chest: "*Your* God killed *my* child!"

These two servants of Abraham are not the heroes of the story. It is the voice of God's angel who saves the day. We, too, are often bystanders. But, if it is true that our perceptions of God change over time, I wonder if we might think of God as speaking today through the earthly voices of servants like you and me. Imagine yourself in following situations: What if you were just doing your job and came across a person struggling with

8. Phillips, *Your God is Too Small*, 23–24.

their faith? What if you just happened to cross paths with someone who needed help spiritually? What would say to the father who has just lost his baby?

I hope you would say that God is good. I hope you would say that God is love. Even more importantly, I pray that you would be present with that person in their need. Abraham's servants stayed with the donkey, but I pray that you would not stay in the car or out in the waiting room. Abraham's servants missed the climax of the drama, but I pray that you would have the courage and the strength to stand by that person's side through the struggles, the doubts, and even the anger directed at God. For it seems to me that this is a real test of faith.

Some sermons end with answers. Today, I will let these questions hang in the air in order to remind us of the mystery of faith and of our responsibility to put our faith into action.

Can you look tragedy in the eye and still believe in God? Can you listen to angry words or take the brunt of a finger pointed at you, and still love your neighbor who bears the image of God? Even if there is nothing to say, can you stand with people who are in pain, in grief, in sorrow? Can you stand such a test of faith?

13

Re-Membering the Future[1]

LIVING WORDS

NEW DUBLIN PRESBYTERIAN WAS founded in 1769. As you might expect from such a historic church, we have about one thousand, seven hundred and sixty-nine traditions. Some are fairly recent, such as singing "God Bless America" on the Fourth of July at the request of a long-time member. Other traditions go back beyond the memory of the living. We do certain things because, "That's the way we've *always* done them." Some of my colleagues lament this familiar refrain in their churches, but I appreciate the history of New Dublin. I have discovered that many of these cherished rituals occur around holidays, such as Holy Week. Based on the etymology of the word, it is fitting for "holy" days to include activities that are "set apart."

I grew up with the tradition of washing graves on Good Friday. Traditionally, Moravian tombstones are squares made out of white marble. Each one is the same size, shape, and color. On Good Friday, families scrub away a year's worth of dirt so that the marble will shine like polished pearls for the traditional Easter sunrise service.

The historic cemetery at New Dublin contains graves of all different shapes and sizes. Many are beautiful in their own right; sadly, a few are in disarray. We do maintain a special bank account as our cemetery fund, but unfortunately, the interest derived from this account does not even cover the cost of professional lawn maintenance. So we save money by hiring an older youth in the church to cut the grass every week. Our church property covers more than nineteen acres, so this is a tradition

1. This terminology is indebted to Paul Galbreath who writes of "re-membering the body of Christ" (Galbreath, *Leading from the Table*, 35).

that also constitutes a demanding rite of passage! But the upkeep of the graves themselves is left to individual families and only a few are willing and able to commit the time and energy necessary for regular maintenance.

Easter, however, is different. All week, the little road to the cemetery hummed with cars kicking up dust clouds, as families made the pilgrimage to the graves of their loved ones. Many of these pilgrims did more than scrubbing and cleaning. As my dog and I strolled through the cemetery, we saw all kinds of items left beside the tombstones: wreaths, flowers, crosses, ceramic angels, even Christmas lights. My dog discovered a *ham biscuit* left lying on top of a tombstone. I do not know if this represented some kind of offering, but I know for a fact that my dog approves of this practice and hopes it becomes a regular tradition!

When I wasn't trying to keep my dog out of the cemetery, I happened to read an article by Lauren Winner about a spiritual discipline she terms, "dislocated exegesis." This rather sophisticated terminology relates to the simple premise that, "Where you read changes how you read."[2] The idea is to move out of places and situations where Scripture is commonly read, such as a church or private study, in order to understand a text in new ways.

During Holy Week, I tried reading the lectionary passages in the cemetery. As I walked around, I read about the women who went to anoint Jesus' body. They, too, brought gifts for the dead, which caused me to think differently about the little memorials scattered among the graves. I watched modern day pilgrims planting flowers as I read about Mary Magdalene mistaking the risen Jesus for a gardener. I discovered that reading the Bible helped me fully enjoy the beauty of our cemetery. Since Easter was relatively late this year, the flowers were in full bloom in the mountains of southwestern Virginia: white dogwood blossoms, yellow forsythia, blue hydrangeas, and redbud. Such brightness and beauty brought to mind scriptures that praise the Creator. As I walked past our memorial butterfly garden, I read, "O Lord, our Sovereign, how majestic is your name in all the earth" (Ps 8:1). I stopped at the top of a ridge overlooking the entire church grounds and read, "O Lord, how manifold are your works! In wisdom you have made them all; the earth is full of your creatures" (Ps 104:24). Dislocated exegesis put a new perspec-

2. Winner, "Dislocated Exegesis," 14.

tive on cherished and time honored lectionary readings. The practice breathed new life into the tradition.

One of the most sacred traditions at New Dublin is the Easter sunrise service. This year, I raised a few eyebrows when I *changed* the format and began the service in the sanctuary. In light of my experience with dislocated exegesis, I wanted to gather our community in the darkness like the women did before visiting Jesus' tomb (Mark 16:1–3). I read the account of those pilgrims' first journey as we processed from the sanctuary to the cemetery, crunching along the gravel parking lot and smelling the freshly cut grass. We stopped at the top of ridge that overlooks the cemetery. Then we read the following from Psalm 113:

(Leader) Blessed be the name of the Lord from this time on and forevermore.

(All) From the rising of the sun to its setting, the name of the Lord be praised.

As if on cue, the sun peeked out from the far horizon. Every grave looked holy in that light.

NEW OLD TRADITIONS

Traditions develop during Holy Week because Easter happens every year. Yet if the biblical accounts of the resurrected Jesus are any indicator, the resurrected body confounds all expectations, traditional and otherwise. Mary Magdalene walked and talked with Jesus. How could she not have recognized his face? If people who personally knew Jesus could not identify him, then we must surmise that the resurrected body is somehow *different*. This may seem obvious.

However, we routinely compare Easter to spring. We have a tendency to think of the resurrection in familiar terms, such as the blossoming of flowers. In so doing, we imply that the resurrection is a seasonal event. In faith, the *opposite* is true. The resurrection breaks the seasonal cycle of life and death. Specifically, the resurrection was a dramatic in-breaking of God into the world. The real beauty of Easter is that God has done something entirely *new*. While this may also seem obvious, it is a message too often lost.

As part of our vacation to Scotland, my family had the opportunity to visit a Scottish Presbyterian church. This little rural church was designed much like mine back in Virginia. It had a raised pulpit in front and a balcony in the back. But instead of pews like New Dublin, the first floor was neatly arranged with modern chairs adorned with soft cushions. When I went upstairs to the balcony, however, I saw the traditional wooden pews. No cushions here! Most likely, this Scottish church is not packing people up to the balcony every Sunday. Perhaps they could not afford to refurnish the entire worship space, but I also think that they could not bear to part completely with tradition, even if some of the old ways had to be regulated to the balcony. It is a challenge to stay true to the past and yet relevant to the present.

I appreciate tradition. I realize that change is difficult. But change can also exceed our expectations. As was the case on the first Easter morning, the new thing that God is doing can be grace. When Mary Magdalene went to the tomb early in the morning, she intended to mourn the past. As soon as she learned that Jesus' body is missing, she wanted to know where they had taken her Lord. She wanted things to return to the way they were, even if that included death. From Mary's frantic search for Jesus' body, we can learn that, even through a period of instability, we can discover God's presence with us. For Mary could not have possibly come to the tomb early enough; God was already waiting for her. The Easter message is about change: death is changed into life.

While the Easter message is a gift, I recognize that such change is also a challenge for churches from Scotland to New Dublin and everywhere else. We must push our assumptions of what it means to be Christian. We may think we know what Jesus looks like, but we should allow ourselves the surprise of new revelations. And so I come back to this idea of dislocated exegesis. Just as visiting another church can yield insights into our own context, new experiences can show us another side of our faith. Instead of automatically falling back into familiar patterns and rituals, we need the courage and the faith to look for new ministry, just as we look forward to new life.

This willingness to change, however, contains a risk as well. Perhaps now more than ever, we are in danger of making an idol out of novelty. I once saw a television commercial that depicted a woman buying a brand new phone, only to walk out of the store and see a billboard advertising an even newer phone! Likewise, we can think that new traditions or services are "must haves." If the only goal is to hear or to do something new, then we have made an idol out of novelty.

Along these lines, Bruce Reyes-Chow, the former moderator of the Presbyterian Church (USA), wrote a blog entry entitled, "Why Churches

Should Stop Making a Big Deal Out of Easter Worship." He observes that many Christians *only* attend church on Easter and writes, "The problem I have is that we too often put on a 'show' for visitors rather than invite them to experience the community that is the church. How powerful would it be to have an Easter worship service that is inspiring, energetic, moving and transformative and be able to say to a visitor or infrequent attendee, 'If you have experienced something profound today, do come back, because this is what is like every Sunday!'"[3]

I think Reyes-Chow makes a great point. Easter is a special day in the life of the church, but even more importantly, Easter points to God's steadfast love that is available to every person, every day of the year. On Easter morning, we are not looking to do something new any more than we merely desire to entertain people. The meaning of Easter is not found in the hoopla or pageantry of our worship services. While we are challenged by the message of change, Easter is only a "big deal" because it is the promise that God is faithful. This is the same steadfast hope, whether Christians confess this belief in 1769 or 2011.

During this year's Holy Week, I had yet another profound experience of dislocated exegesis. Joel is a retired man with a full-time hobby. One afternoon, he showed me his elaborate model city in the basement of his townhouse. There is a drugstore, a school, a church, and model train tracks encircling all these buildings. Joel can operate several locomotives at once, skillfully guiding them to avoid a collision. Part of me wishes that life could be as easy to control as it is in Joel's basement. I would love to direct New Dublin into the future, but sometimes it seems as if the love of tradition and the necessity of change are on a collision course from opposite ends of the same track.

In real life, Joel has endured his share of pain and loss. He has not created this model city in order to escape from reality. He explained to me that his father loved steam locomotives. His interest in model trains began as a way to bring back memories of his childhood with his dad. In his basement, Joel has created something new in order to remember the best of the past as comfort and as inspiration for the future. He teaches me that traditions can be open to change. Like building a model city, we can add new layers of meaning to existing rituals and ideas. In this process, our remembrance of the past is strengthened, not negated. Perhaps this is a model for the church.

3. Reyes-Chow, "Why Churches Should Stop," lines 33–37.

PURE GOLD

This year, we celebrated confirmation on Easter. While this was not the tradition at New Dublin, the idea was not new. The ancient church received new members through baptism on the night of the Easter vigil. For us, it was a new old tradition, but the significance related to the value of relationships.

Before we received our youth into adult membership in our church, I had the privilege of teaching confirmation class. Our youth are bright young men and women. As the class progressed and we built trust in one another, they became more inquisitive. They wanted to know about the session. Why do the elders get to make decisions on behalf of the rest of the congregation? They were also curious about other churches. Why aren't women ordained as elders and pastors in other denominations? And they asked about theology and ritual. Why do some churches sprinkle babies with water and others immerse adults? I tried my best to answer all of these questions, and we had some wonderful conversations.

I think, however, that the confirmation students learned more through their relationships with their mentors. In addition to my class, each youth was paired with an adult in the church. This system worked very well. In fact, the culture of southern Appalachia truly values the idea of apprenticeship. I see evidence all the time between farmers, session members, and teachers. Tex Sample believes that rural churches in particular should tap into existing structures in the community that have existed for generations. One example is when a novice learns through tutelage under an experienced mentor. Education takes place outside of the traditional classroom and teaching takes place through shared experiences.[4]

Mentorship also relates to the daily practice of discipleship; we must teach others to live their faith every day. The confirmation class reminded me of this truth in powerful ways. It was a blessing to have a regular meeting time to talk about our faith, to think about tough questions, and to pray together. I learned who had just hit a homerun and who had baby chicks, whose horse had a leg infection and whose grandmother was struggling with her health. I learned how to pray for others, when to appreciate another's blessings, and, most especially, about the gift of trust. I was the teacher, but my faith was strengthened by these relationships with the students.

4. Sample, *Ministry in an Oral Culture*, 16–19.

While it is wonderful to celebrate special holidays, each day is an opportunity to grow and to learn. The Christian life is not simply an extended prelude to Easter's Hallelujah chorus! We need reminders of our faith throughout the year. The grace that we extend to one another may even give us a glimpse of God. In the beautiful Saint John's Bible, the illuminations of various biblical scenes are often interspersed with real gold. Throughout the books of the Bible, gold represents the presence of God. Sometimes the gold is arranged into squares that are polished to the point that you can see your reflection in them. God is in you; God is among us.

In their confirmation service, I wanted to reflect this idea of God's presence in our relationships. Based on my knowledge of their faith and their lives, I selected a Bible verse for each student that I hoped would speak personally to them. This practice of selecting a "watchword" of Scripture is yet another tradition from my Moravian heritage. I vividly remember my father reciting my confirmation watchword with his hand upon my forehead: "'For surely I know the plans I have for you,' says the Lord, 'Plans for your welfare and not for harm, to give you a future with hope'" (Jer 29:11). I hope that their watchwords will be equally as memorable. Though it was a new ritual, I pray that they will remember their experience of confirmation as a time when they saw the love of God in other faces of their community of faith.

To this day, Ginny and I laugh about our dog's discovery of the ham biscuit in the graveyard. Talk about a golden discovery! While no such offering has appeared again, we think that she still hunts for another treat. And who could blame her? We humans look to recapture powerful experiences from our past as well. This is the heart of tradition: bringing meaning to the present by remembering the past.

Yet we do ourselves a disservice by living exclusively in the past. Much has been made about the loss of young people in mainline denominations, but I believe that we can reach out to youth without new services or new music or new ideas. We can "re-member the future" by bringing new *members* into our churches through building relationships that model Christian community and reflect God's love. This is a message for cherishing the past and exploring the present in order to shape the future. This is an emphasis on sacred memories and new experiences. This is Easter *and* this is our faith on every other day.

"CELEBRATE THE WAIT"

April 24th, 2011
John 20:1–18

My friends, the Lord is risen! Yes, the Lord is risen indeed!

This morning, we have much to celebrate. This is Easter! And, in just a moment, eight young men and women will come to the front of the church and profess their faith. They are going to claim the baptismal promises for themselves.

And all God's *parents* said, "Amen!"

If I may speak directly to our confirmation class, let me assure you that we have all been waiting and praying for this day. It is one thing for you to hear that Jesus loves you and that nothing can separate you from the love of God, but quite another thing for you to feel this love in your own unique and personal way. We have waited for you to *confirm* this faith for yourself.

The beauty of today's gospel reading lies in such a confirmation of faith. Mary Magdalene recognizes Jesus for herself; Jesus speaks directly to her. It is an experience that she has and that no one else can have for her. Jesus says her name and she confirms her faith.

Perhaps you noticed, however, some *differences* between Mary's confirmation and your own experience. While she only went to a garden one time, you had to go for months to class at the church. This difference can be explained by the fact that Mary had the risen Lord as her teacher, but you were stuck with me!

Seriously, what can we all learn from Mary's experience that will help us along our faith journey? It seems to me that we can draw several conclusions from her example:

Like Mary, we *believe* in the resurrection. We proclaim the good news that Jesus Christ is risen from the dead. Just as was true for the first disciples, our belief in the resurrection is a special kind of knowledge. What you *believe* is not necessarily what you *think*. To believe means "to give your heart."[5] Such belief is not a scientific process of hypothesis, observation, and conclusion. We believe that a love greater than us reaches out to us. We cannot explain this love; we cannot "prove" it. But we can believe; indeed, we can only believe.

5. Norris, *Amazing Grace*, 62.

This difference between knowledge and belief is an important part of our Scripture lesson. How can it be that Mary didn't recognize Jesus? She walked with Jesus, witnessed his healings, heard him preach, broke bread with him—surely, she would instantly recognize his face! But in fact, she must wait for Jesus to reveal himself. The risen Christ is not something than can be proved; it is a belief that must be given. This is grace. We cannot earn it or control it. We must wait for God.

Now I am aware that ours is the culture of microwave meals and high speed internet. We don't like to wait, do we? Well, take heart: it is true that we celebrate our confirmation class *today*. In just a moment, one kind of wait will be over. They will be members of our church, New Dublin Presbyterian!

But they are also a part of God's universal church that covers the whole world and stretches throughout history. As part of the body of Christ, we are all waiting for the final consummation of God's kingdom on earth. We are waiting for the ultimate celebration when God lives among us, just as Jesus walked our earth (Rev 21:3). My friends, this is something that only God can do. We can confirm new members to our church; but we must wait for God to establish heaven on earth. Waiting for God, then, is waiting with *hope*.

But it is also true that we have things to do while we wait. We wait as we break bread during Holy Communion and at fellowship suppers. We wait as we sing hymns on Easter morning and at the funeral services of our loved ones. We wait as we visit the sick in the hospital and the victims of tornadoes in shelters.

So here is my challenge to the confirmation class: remember our friend Mary Magdalene. After her confirmation experience, she ran to tell the rest of the disciples the good news (John 20:18). The belief that she confirmed inspired her to act; may it be true of you as well. We need your energy and your ideas. We need your perspective and your insights into the world. We have a rich and beautiful tradition at New Dublin; will you become a part of it? Will you build on what we have been by being who you are?

Belief should lead to action. I think that our confirmation students understand this concept. When we were in class, it was clear that you learned more through your participation. Oh sure, I could tell you what I thought (and you were polite enough to listen). But the most memorable lessons came from your mentors, didn't they? I told you about the ministry of elders; you learned when your mentor drove you to visit the sick. I told you about the importance of fellowship; you learned by going to your mentor's house after school. I told you that God loves you; you learned by experiencing these loving relationships.

Now that your wait to become a member is about to be over, the challenge will be to build on these lessons. Your mentors, your pastor, and your church family all want to learn from you as well. Will you build on what we have been by being who you are? We are counting on you for there is much work to be done.

Ernest Hemingway once told a story of a Spanish father who decided to reconcile with his runaway son. This father hadn't spoken to his son in years, but knew that he was somewhere in the city of Madrid. Therefore, he took out an ad in the largest newspaper: "Paco, meet me at Hotel Montana at noon on Tuesday. All is forgiven. Love, Papa." Paco, however, is a common name in Spain, and when this father arrived at the hotel, he saw over eight hundred Pacos! Each son was anxiously awaiting his estranged father.

You see, the world is waiting for reconciliation. So today, we proclaim our belief in the message of Easter: our greatest hope is that death is not the end. We believe; we give our hearts to God. Christ the Lord is risen today! Hallelujah!

And today, we celebrate the wait. We all wait with hope for what God will do in the future because of what God has done in the past. We hope for reconciliation because of Jesus' resurrection. We celebrate that God has called new men and women of all ages into our midst to do the work of God's kingdom and help a hurting world.

Join us, confirmation class, so that we can learn from one another. By God's grace, build on what we have been by being who you are.

14

Any Last Words?

STANDING ON HOLY GROUND

O N MAY 24TH, MY Dad called. I assumed he was going to wish Ginny a happy birthday. I could not have been more wrong. He said that my granddad lay dying in a hospice house in North Carolina.

We had known for months that Granddad's prostate cancer had spread all over his body and seeped into his bones. But no one, including his doctors, was prepared for him to go downhill so quickly. Over the phone, however, Dad made it clear that he was near the end of life. Ginny and I got into the car.

Having almost completed a year in ministry, I already had become well-acquainted with the particular look of a person in hospice care: mouth open, lips cracked, skin oily. Each person also has this distant look in his or her eyes. Dad describes this gaze as "looking into the world beyond." Perhaps it is only due to the morphine. But like my father, I have an intuitive sense any person with this look sees something that the rest of us do not.

Previous experience notwithstanding, I was still unprepared to see my granddad with this hospice look. From the time of my childhood, I remember the big wide smile on his face. He faithfully served as a Moravian minister for decades, but I think that the beauty of his life was his childlike joy for the world around him and, most especially, for other people. When they learned of his death, several of my parishioners told me that they still remembered Granddad from his visit to New Dublin at my ordination, even though that service had taken place over a year ago. I, too, was grateful for those memories, especially recalling that he stood next to me for my ordination as I sat next to his death bed.

Since he could exude such childlike joy, perhaps it was fitting that Granddad died in a childlike state. My cousin who sat vigil with us noted the circularity of life: we are born as creatures in total dependence and, at least in hospice, we die with the same dependence upon others. There is nothing like death to put things into perspective. Though Granddad died in a palliative care room, there was no morphine to numb the emotional pain of his family or blur our sense of loss. As difficult as it was to watch a loved one die, perhaps the greatest blessing was being confronted with the sheer, raw emotions. I have found it to be true that certain moments in the process of dying are nothing short of beautiful, the kind of spiritual experience that makes you want to take your shoes off when standing on this holy ground.

When I first walked into Granddad's room, his gaunt, pained expression took my breath away. I briefly considered stepping back out into the hallway to compose myself, but Dad had just announced my entrance: "Andrew's here."

Granddad opened his eyes, which were at that moment bluer than any blue I have seen.

An electric shock ran up my spine.

"I love you, Granddad," I said, tears spilling down my cheeks.

He mouthed, I love you, I love you, I love you. No sound. His lips formed a holy Trinitarian formula. I love you, I love you, I love you.

After that dramatic moment, he mostly slept. People visited and we talked. We ate. We took turns holding his hands and dabbing Vaseline on his dry, cracked lips. We prayed often, mostly in silence and with deep breaths. Time dragged by. Time flew away.

As the hour approached for our departure, Dad suggested that we have a formal prayer. We gathered around Granddad's bed with the rest of the family. As I am accustomed to do, I looked at Dad for leadership. As he is accustomed to do, Dad took charge and led us in the reading of Scripture. Then Ginny agreed to lead the singing of "Amazing Grace."

As soon as we lifted up those first notes, Granddad roused himself from the morphine induced fog. His toes moved in time with the tune and, once again, his lips soundlessly formed words, this time that beautifully familiar verse: I once was lost, but now I'm found.

Take my word: you would have wanted to take off your shoes.

SEEING A LITTLE LIGHT

As a pastor, I want to do death well. First of all, I want to know the person who is dying. Long before death's doorstep, I want to have talked politics, shared iced tea, and learned all the names of the grandchildren. I want to have laughed and prayed together. As my granddad taught me, life is sanctified by such relationships. Near the end, I want to be present in the hospital or the hospice room. I want to be there for the spouse, the siblings, and the children. I want to be there on behalf of New Dublin Presbyterian Church. I want to be there to put my hand on the dying brow and whisper the benediction. After death, I want to write the eulogy.

I distinctly remember being warned against the practice of writing eulogies in seminary. Presbyterians, I was told, do not wax about the deceased at funerals. We preach at the Service of Witness to the Resurrection. Though ordained Presbyterian, I am nonetheless very Moravian in my love of eulogies. In the Moravian tradition, the eulogy is actually called the Lebenslauf, a term that could be translated as "a life's path" or "journey of life." Granddad once told me that every Moravian was supposed to write his or her own Lebenslauf over the course of a life, much like a memoir, and leave only the closing remarks to be filled in by the pastor at death. While this may have been the ideal, Granddad knew all too well from his experience that the pastor researches, writes, and delivers the eulogy at the funeral service.

So it seems to me that my preference for eulogies is derived even more from my family history than any denomination. My dad does death well and he learned from my granddad. I have learned how to write and deliver a eulogy from them, mostly through observation. It's true, I think, that younger pastors learn through osmosis, soaking up the lessons from their elders just by being in their presence. This is especially true if the senior pastor is your father or grandfather.

For any eulogy, my goal is to give an accurate description of the life of the deceased that glorifies God, rather than deifies the dead. Each one of us is created in the image of God. I think of a eulogy as a snapshot of a life in which God shines around the silhouette, as the sun rises behind a person on a hill.

My first Service of Witness to the Resurrection did not include a planned eulogy. I was a pulpit supply pastor for the summer before I began my studies at the University of Virginia, and an elderly woman died in that congregation. Truthfully, I did not want to conduct this service and even asked a local pastor to substitute. I had never met this woman, so I figured that one pastor was as good as the next. But when I spoke with the family, they assured me that they wanted a brief service. Well shoot, I remember thinking, I can do that!

The day came and I led a very brief service in the funeral home. I read Scripture and prayed. We all sang a hymn and headed out to the gravesite. One of the elders of that church rode with me. After a few remarks about the weather (he didn't like the heat) and the style of my car (he did like the model), he wanted to know why I had not said some words about her life. I looked at him sideways and impatiently told him that the family had requested a brief service. He looked out the window and was silent for the rest of the trip.

We arrived at the graveyard eventually and I stood beside the coffin, waiting for the pallbearers to bring the casket from the hearse. That's when it dawned on me that the "brief service" requested by the family probably included the expectation of a few brief remarks about the deceased. My palms became very sweaty with that realization. Already I could hear the inevitable complaints after the service: "The pastor didn't seem to even know her!" I looked down at my folder; there were beautiful words on the page. But I knew darn well that the most elegant liturgy will sound hollow if it rings of impersonal formality. Looking out at the friends and family of a dead woman I had never met, I tried to think of what Granddad would do.

Before I read those beautiful words of the liturgy, I spoke about my first tour of their church. As I walked through the education wing, it was pointed out that this woman had made all of the curtains for the children's classrooms. She had picked out the material and sewn the curtains by hand. While she had no grandchildren of her own, she insisted on making those curtains as a gift to future generations. In fact, she was kind of like that all of her life. She was willing to put time and energy into the little details, not for credit, but for the benefit of others—especially children. If we would only pull back the curtain a little to view her life, we would see that God's love shone through her.

In so many words, that was my first eulogy—an impromptu one no less! That was also my first experience conducting a Service of Witness to the Resurrection. By my own standards, I did not do this death very well. But after it was all over, her only surviving son came up to me in the fellowship hall and shook my hand.

"You did a great job," he said. "Mom would have been so pleased."

Then he added, "I thought that you said that you'd never met her? How did you know what she was like?"

Ever since that day, I have been aware of curtains and millions of other seemingly insignificant things that tell the story of a person's life. Ultimately, these details constitute a part of God's great story of redemption—the light shining behind each one of our lives.

PREACHING A EULOGY

I want to conclude this chapter by sharing a few things that I have learned about the process of preaching a eulogy.

First of all, it is very important for a pastor to meet with the family of the deceased before the service. During this time, I try to give space for people to share stories and memories. Whether these accounts are funny or sad, profound or quotidian, I frequently witness a cathartic effect among the loved ones as they speak of the deceased. The days immediately after a death can be chaotic, full of things to do and people to see. It can be a holy activity to set time apart just to remember together.

These stories that come out of the family meeting are typically included in my eulogy. But pastors need to exercise caution to avoid glorifying a person instead of God. I have found that it is helpful to use Scripture as a bridle for the family's comments. As part of the meeting with the family, I specifically ask if there are certain biblical passages that were favorites of the deceased or specific texts that come to mind when thinking about his or her life. Not only does recalling Scripture add a spiritual element to this time of remembrance, but these passages serve as the basis for the eulogy itself. In order to prevent the funeral service from bounding down trails of human glorification or idolatry, I reign in my words in light of these selected biblical passages.

I structured one eulogy around Psalm 23. As I read each line, I noted an intersection between the image found in the psalm and the life of the deceased. As the psalmist imagines a table being spread out before his enemies (Ps 23:5), I spoke of this particular woman's penchant for cooking extra portions. In her own words, she always made enough food for "the man in the woods," meaning any person in need who might happen to stop by. I believe that the image in Psalm 23:5 is one of reconciliation: there can be healing and forgiveness in the sharing of food from the same table. As a Christian, this is true of the Lord's Table and the sharing of Holy Communion. In the eulogy, I connected these ideas as a way to honor the life of the deceased and inspire us to "cook for the man in the woods."

This raises another important aspect of a eulogy: the words about the dead are heard by the living. A eulogy can bring comfort and healing. There was a man at New Dublin who died after a long and difficult struggle with his health. When I met with his widow the following morning, she spoke of her sense of relief. She recalled Jesus' famous line about his easy yoke and his light burden (Matt 11:30). In that eulogy, I preached that a burden had been lifted and a baptism had been made complete in death. The yoke is easy, the burden is light, and now, the rest is complete. His widow requested a copy of that eulogy, and she tells me that she often rereads it. Thanks be to God, I believe that I did that death well.

I did not preach a eulogy, read Scripture, or have any formal part in Granddad's service. I was one of his grandsons, the only role I wanted to be. But I did mention Granddad's life as part of the sermon I preached exactly one year after my first Sunday at New Dublin. It seems fitting that those remarks are included in the final sermon of this collection, *Take My Hand*. But I have one last image of my first year that I'd like to share first. To do so, we must go back to my granddad's hospice room.

After we sang "Amazing Grace" with Granddad mouthing the words, everyone felt the holiness of that moment. Then everyone looked at my dad to tell us what to do next. I know I did. But this time Dad did not take charge.

"Well, Rev. Taylor-Troutman," he said smiling, "that is about as perfect a lead into prayer as I've ever experienced!"

I nodded, also smiling, agreeing with him.

Suddenly, I realized that he meant for me to pray!

I bowed my head and took a deep breath. Silence. Granddad struggled for another raspy breath. More silence. My wife squeezed my hand. You can do it, she seemed to say. Then the words came—truthfully, I hardly remember what I prayed. But I believe that I was prepared to offer that prayer by serving over the past year. Though I have learned a great deal about preaching eulogies, I have learned even more from preaching on a weekly basis in a variety of situations to this growing community of faith. As a eulogy comes out of the life of a person, so my sermons come from my experience of the people of New Dublin. And I'm still learning. I think that Granddad would be proud. For that, I am grateful beyond words.

"A LIFETIME OF LEARNING"

May 29th, 2011
Acts 17:22–31

If we were to read the entire book of Acts up to today's lesson, we would discover the power of the gospel to reach different kinds of people: rich and poor, Jew and gentile, slave and free, male and female. As Paul preaches in Athens, however, we are confronted with another question: Can the gospel hold its own in a university town?[1]

Just as the University of Virginia is a bastion of the Enlightenment philosophers, Athens was the central location of the great thinkers of its culture. From ancient times, the Areopagus had been the central meeting place of this urban intelligentsia. The name, Areopagus, literally means "the hill of Ares," referring to the Greek god of war. But the "battles" fought there were mostly mental—this is the kind of intellectual activity, which our narrator Luke refers to rather pejoratively as "people spending their time in nothing but telling or hearing something new" (Acts 17:21).[2]

As a recent graduate of the University of Virginia, I am acutely aware of the suspicion that the university is nothing but a bunch of long-winded folk who like to hear the sound of their own voices. Before I went to seminary, various people warned me against losing my religion in the process of my studies. In Jesus' day, there were concerns about Nazareth; but we ask in our culture if anything good can come from the academy! Perhaps some of this caution is warranted. In certain circles, there is a fear that new scholarship will undermine the foundations of the old and sacred faith. There are some scholars who do seek to do precisely this.

Yet there is another way as well—a blending of faith and intellect as conversation partners. Case in point: Paul's sermon to the Athenians is a

1. Willimon, Acts, 142.
2. Gonzalez, Acts, 201.

beautiful illustration of a learned scholar presenting the Christian faith. In this sermon, Paul shows his mastery of the ancient art of rhetoric or public-speaking. He begins by praising his audience, insisting that they are very religious people (Acts 17:22). This sort of laudable introduction was known as the captatio benevolentiae, and it was a form of address as sophisticated as it sounds.[3]

Then Paul makes an appeal to what is known as "natural theology," meaning that our observation of nature is a forerunner to faith in a Creator.[4] In making this academic argument, Paul sprinkles in quotations from the poet Epimenides of Crete and the Stoic philosophers Cleanthes and Aratus. Even Paul's criticism of images made from gold, silver, or stone finds a similar echo in a sixth-century philosopher from Athens named Xenophanes.[5]

This morning, I reference this scholarship to show that Paul was conversant with the classical as well as the current philosophies of his day. His faith in the resurrection of Jesus Christ was not threatened by so-called pagan or secular knowledge. He did not lose his religion in his studies. In fact, Paul's knowledge actually strengthened his faith. He did not shy away from the Areopagus or shrink from a battle of the minds, but actively engaged great thinkers by using their own textbooks. Instead of seeing the academy as attacking religion, Paul supported his arguments with knowledge from the prominent philosophies of the culture.

I thought about this positive dynamic between faith and intellect this week, as I watched my grandfather die. Up until the last weeks of his life, Granddad was still reading the latest biblical scholarship and listening to lecture series from today's top religion professors. Not only was he intelligent, Granddad was committed to staying current and dedicated to studying even in his retirement. In fact, I remember a rather embarrassing moment during the Christmas break after my first semester in seminary. Granddad asked me about my studies, and I rather arrogantly boasted of having read the newest book of a particularly outstanding scholar. I simply assumed that he had never heard of this modern scholarship. As I finished summarizing the book, however, Granddad gently told me how to correctly pronounce the author's last name!

3. Ibid., 202.
4. Willimon, *Acts*, 143.
5. Gonzalez, *Acts*, 202.

Granddad believed that acquiring knowledge can be a good, even a holy, quest. Like Paul converted certain disciples after his speech in Athens, so people are influenced in positive ways by new scholarship and by new learning. New teaching can have lasting impacts.

As I sat beside my granddad's hospice bed, a parade of pastors came to pay their respects. These clergy were learned and trained in their own right, but they spoke of my granddad as their role model and their teacher. Lay people wrote cards that specifically mentioned lessons that Granddad had taught and how much that learning meant to their faith. There was one particular gentleman who is currently on the religious faculty at a major university and has authored at least a dozen books. In his note, he said that my granddad was the first person who showed him that it was possible to be both a scholar and a pastor—a thinker and a person of faith.

As these tributes to my granddad made clear, people are grateful for new ways to think about their faith. Most people are not threatened by knowledge. They are inspired to live their lives in new and meaningful ways. Whether or not we live in a university town and teach on a university faculty, we all have faith to think about. Like Paul, we have a responsibility to engage the culture around us. We all have our own Areopagus. We should not ask people to turn off their brains when they enter our sanctuary. We should encourage them to think seriously about their faith and equip them with the best knowledge available. Learning about our faith is a life-long process, from our earliest memories of baptism to the eventual day when our baptism will be completed in death.

I had a conversation this past week with a very special little girl who is going to be baptized in just a few weeks. How do you teach the meaning of baptism to someone so young? We began by talking about water; she knew so much about water! You can play in water, wash the dirt off your hands, and give your dog a bath. We talked about how we drink water and how the rain waters plants so that we can eat them.

Then I made a comparison: just as water does all these wonderful things for us, so the water of baptism represents the wonderful things that God is doing. God cleans us up and quenches our thirst; God nourishes our bodies and our hearts. I realized that this is rather abstract thinking, but my young friend understood the main point.

"I'm learning," she said with a laugh. "Learning, learning, learning!"

We can study in universities, in Sunday school, and in small groups. We can learn doctrines and dogmas, theories and philosophies. But the goal is not to simply learn something new. In fact, it seems to me that the stakes are much higher.

We live in a culture where intellect and faith are increasingly seen as hostile to the other by both sides. Instead of listening to these voices, may we be open to the idea that faith and intellect can be conversation partners. As Paul spoke in the Areopagus, may we bring the gospel into different places and times. And in so doing, may we rediscover, time and time again, the child-like joy in grasping a new insight—the joy of learning, learning, learning.

Epilogue

The End of Our Beginning

I WROTE THIS BOOK over the course of my first year at New Dublin. The sermons, of course, took a great deal of focused energy each week, usually for hours on end. But the reflections were written in mostly twenty minute intervals at the end of my day. For a long time, this book was just a file on my home computer entitled, "Journal."

When the time came to submit my work for publication, I had to think of an actual title. Originally, I came up with, *It Seems to Me: Reflections and Sermons from the First Year of a Parish Pastor*. I liked this title because it was descriptive. My writing group at the Collegeville Institute, however, unanimously agreed that it was boring. In fact, one of my colleagues said she wouldn't buy a book with that title, not even as a gift for her boring aunt! Well, I hope that she in particular likes *Take My Hand*.

I eventually settled on this title, however, because it, too, is descriptive of the journey and simultaneously issues an invitation. To return to an idea found in the introduction, I consider myself to be, like Martin Buber, someone who has seen something and who goes to a window and points to what he has seen. When I look at the world, whether through the window of my office or my car or a hospital, I am so often confronted with pain and injustice. Yet I write and preach about a God whose love is more powerful than this daily and constant suffering. While I have drawn some conclusions, this is really a book about questions: Who is God? Where is God? What are we supposed to do with our lives? How can we love and support one another? While specifically addressed in chapter twelve, with the mystery of God's loving presence in a violent world is in the background of almost every single sermon. D. H. Lawrence once said, "I am mad for the unknown." Though certainly not as good a writer

143

as Lawrence, this work proves that I am just as crazy! I am comfortable with the mystery of questions.

I think that I can live with the unknown, however, because I have the love of supportive people. My family is my rock; my wife is my anchor. I could never drift into true madness because I always *know* their love. Likewise, New Dublin is an incredible place to live into my faith. We are partners in ministry. They teach their teacher; they pastor to their pastor. I will always remember their support when I came into this presbytery. Since I was not ordained, I had to preach in the opening worship service before the entire assembly. While I knew that my presbytery is really not that big, it seemed like a cast of thousands! As I stepped into the pulpit that morning, I don't recall ever being so nervous. But then I saw BJ, smiling at me from the back pew of the church. I looked again: New Dublin members had filled up *four* pews! They had traveled for miles on a Thursday morning to show their support. And so, I took a deep breath and preached. Now I have the honor of doing the same thing almost every Sunday. I may be mad for the unknown, but I am grateful to know such love—love that listens patiently; love that seeks a truth bigger than any opinion; love that stays with the questions.

As I suggested in chapter twelve, our lives are filled with "runaway bulls" that we call tornadoes, earthquakes, famines, and genocides. I maintain that we cannot know the reasons why these tragedies occur; yet we believe in an all-knowing and all-powerful God of love. It seems to me that the only way I can keep these polarities together is in a community. I cannot explain the mystery, but I can maintain relationships. I cannot penetrate the unknown, but I can surround myself with people who live the questions. One thing I do know is that I can preach because of the supportive community called New Dublin Presbyterian Church.

Every time I preach, I close the service by offering a charge and benediction. The parishioners might beg to differ, but I admit that I do this closing act very poorly. I have difficulty with endings! Instead of wrapping up our worship with a concise and pithy summation, I sort of babble on, rehashing some of the major points of my sermon. Then I realize that I need to cut it short and end up chopping off my thought midway. At Ginny's urging, I've tried to write the charge and practice it in advance. Hopefully, I have gotten a little better with practice, but I honestly don't think that I will ever do this well. There is part of me that simply doesn't want the service to end. When I look at the congregation of New Dublin, I want to continue to think and preach and laugh and pray with them. Even when I have lemonade on the lawn to look forward to, I don't want to let them go home!

Truthfully, I don't want this book to end either. The folder on my home computer labeled "Journal" records more stories of inspiration and struggle and laughter and tears. I'd like to tell you more about Richard, BJ, and Grace. There are more youth events to report and special services to describe. There are many more "bloopers" to share from our worship services. (Like the time I wanted to describe a group of people "leaping like frogs," only I actually said "clapping like frogs"!)

But this book was never meant to encapsulate all of New Dublin Presbyterian Church. You would learn more by visiting one Sunday than I could tell in a thousand pages. This book was written to encourage you to think about your faith. I could tell you more stories from New Dublin, but the point is that the questions of the unknown can never really be answered—only considered anew by you in your community of faith.

So while I do not know much about good endings, I do know how to tell a story written by Carson Brisson, one of my former professors at Union Presbyterian Seminary.[1]

Once upon a time there was a village where there lived a student who desired to learn and a rabbi who delighted to learn. One spring, student came to rabbi, who was seated, and said, "To learn is my desire."

"And what would you learn?" rabbi asked.

Student replied, "The story of God's own heart."

Rabbi, hearing this, wept, and said to student, "Go away. Listen more. Then return."

The next spring, student came to rabbi, who was seated, and said, "To learn is my desire."

"And what would you learn?" rabbi asked.

Student replied, "Each word of the story of God's own heart."

Rabbi, hearing this, wept, and said to student, "Go away. Listen more. Then return."

The next spring, student came to rabbi, who was seated, and said, "To learn is my desire."

"And what would you learn?" rabbi asked.

1. Brisson, "Slow Joy," 23.

Student replied, "Each letter of each word of the story of God's own heart."

Rabbi, hearing this, wept, and said to student, "Go away. Listen more. Then return."

The next spring, student came to rabbi, who was seated, and said, "To learn is my desire."

"And what would you learn?" rabbi asked.

Student, replied, "Each space between each letter of each word of the story of God's own heart."

Rabbi, hearing this, *stood* and began to sing softly, "So now we can begin."

As he sang, he began to dance, "So now we can begin, so now we can begin, so now we can begin!"

That is as good a benediction as I've ever heard and could ever hope to offer.

Bibliography

Barnes, Craig M. *The Pastor as Minor Poet: Texts and Subtexts in the Ministerial Life.* Grand Rapids: Eerdmans, 2009.

———. *Sacred Thirst: Meeting God in the Desert of Our Longings.* Grand Rapids: Zondervan, 2001.

Bell, Rob. *Love Wins: A Book about Heaven, Hell, and the Fate of Every Person Who Ever Lived.* New York: HarperOne, 2011.

Berry, Wendell. *Jayber Crow: A Novel.* Berkeley: Counterpoint, 2000.

———. *Bringing It to the Table: On Farming and Food.* Berkeley: Counterpoint, 2009.

Bonhoeffer, Dietrich. *The Cost of Discipleship.* 2nd ed. Translated by R. H. Fuller. New York: MacMillan, 1959.

Brisson, Carson E. "Slow Joy." *Focus* 22 (Winter 2010): 23.

Calvin, John. *Institutes of the Christian Religion.* Edited by John T. McNeill. Translated by Ford Lewis Battles. Library of Christian Classics 20, 21. Louisville: Westminster John Knox, 1960.

Cleave, Chris. *Little Bee: A Novel.* New York: Simon & Schuster, 2008.

Coffin, William Sloane. "Alex's Death." In *A Chorus of Witnesses: Sermons for Today's Preacher,* edited by Thomas G. Long and Cornelius Plantinga Jr., 263–266. Grand Rapids: Eerdmans, 1994.

Cook, Michael J. *Muhammad.* Oxford: Oxford University Press, 1996.

Craddock, Fred B. *As One Without Authority: Essays on Inductive Preaching.* Rev. ed. Enid, OK: The Phillips University Press, 1974.

Doidge, Norman. *The Brain That Changes Itself: Stories of Personal Triumph from the Frontiers of Brain Science.* London: Penguin, 2007.

Galbreath, Paul. *Leading from the Table.* Herndon, VA: The Alban Institute, 2008.

Gilbert, Elizabeth. *Eat, Pray, Love: One Woman's Search for Everything Across Italy, India and Indonesia.* New York: Penguin, 2006.

Goldman, Francisco. "The Gospel According to Matthew." In *Revelations: Personal Responses To the Books of the Bible,* 203–213. New York: Canongate, 2005.

Gonzalez, Justo L. *Acts: The Gospel of the Spirit.* Maryknoll, NY: Orbis, 2001.

Guthrie, Shirley C., Jr. *Christian Doctrine.* Rev. ed. Louisville: Westminster John Knox, 1994.

Jacobs, A. J. *The Year of Living Biblically: One Man's Humble Quest to Follow the Bible as Literally as Possible.* New York: Simon & Schuster, 2007.

Kabir. "The Time Before Death." Translated by Robert Bly. In *Ten Poems to Change Your Life,* by Roger Housden. New York: Harmony, 2001.

Keating, Thomas. *Intimacy with God.* New York: Crossroad, 1996.

LaHaye, Tim F., and Jerry B. Jenkins. *Left Behind Collection: Boxed Set Vol. 1–5.* Wheaton, IL: Tyndale, 2003.

Lamott, Anne. *Imperfect Birds: A Novel.* New York: Penguin, 2010.

Lapidus, Ira M. *A History of Islamic Societies*. 2nd ed. Cambridge: Cambridge University Press, 2002.

Lischer, Richard. *Open Secrets: A Memoir of Faith and Discovery*. New York: Broadway, 2001.

Lodahl, Michael. *Claiming Abraham: Reading the Bible and the Qur'an Side by Side*. Grand Rapids: Brazos, 2010.

Long, Thomas G. *The Witness of Preaching*. 2nd ed. Louisville: Westminster John Knox, 2005.

Miles, Sara. *Take This Bread: A Radical Conversion*. New York: Ballantine, 2008.

Norris, Kathleen. *Amazing Grace: A Vocabulary of Faith*. New York: Riverhead, 1998.

Ochs, Peter. "Another Enlightenment." *Christian Century* 128 (2011): 28–32.

———. *Another Reformation: Postliberal Christianity and the Jews*. Grand Rapids: Brazos, 2011.

Peterson, Eugene H. "My Father's Butcher Shop." *Christian Century* 128 (2011): 28–33.

Phillips, J. B. *Your God is Too Small: A Guide for Believers and Skeptics Alike*. New York: Simon & Schuster, 1952.

Pickthall, Mohammed Marmaduke. *The Glorious Qur'an Translation*. 2nd ed. Elmhurst, NY: Tahrike Tarsile Qur'an, 2003.

Reyes-Chow, Bruce. "Why Churches Should Stop Making a Big Deal Out of Easter Worship." No pages. Online: http://www.huffingtonpost.com/bruce-reyeschow /why-churches-should-stop-_b_843880.html. Accessed April 5, 2011.

Rilke, Rainer Maria. *Letters to a Young Poet*. 2nd ed. Translated by Joan M. Burnham. Novato, CA: New World Library, 2000.

Ringe, Sharon H. *Luke*. Westminster Bible Companion. Louisville: Westminster John Knox, 1995.

Robinson, Marilynne. *Gilead: A Novel*. New York: Picador, 2004.

Rossing, Barbara "The So-Called Rapture." In *Journeys Through Revelation: Apocalyptic Hope for Today*, 81–82. Horizons Bible Study 23/3. Louisville: Presbyterian Women (PCUSA), 2010.

Sample, Tex. *Ministry in an Oral Culture: Living with Will Rogers, Uncle Remus, and Minnie Pearl*. Louisville: Westminster John Knox, 1994.

Schleiermacher, Friedrich. *The Christian Faith*. Edited by H. R. MacKintosh and J. S. Steward. London: T & T Clark, 1999.

Solomon, Norman. *Judaism: A Brief Insight*. New York: Sterling, 1996.

Taylor, Barbara Brown. *Leaving Church: A Memoir of Faith*. New York: HarperOne, 2006.

Volf, Miroslav. *Exclusion and Embrace: A Theological Exploration of Identity, Otherness, and Reconciliation*. Nashville: Abingdon, 1996.

Willimon, William H. *Acts*. Interpretation: A Bible Commentary for Teaching and Preaching. Atlanta: John Knox, 1988.

Winner, Lauren. "Dislocated Exegesis." *Christian Century* 128 (2011): 13–14.